# Testimonials

As parents of two young children and regular EFT users, we greatly appreciate the value and importance of Sharon's work. We wholeheartedly recommend her new book *Heal Your Birth, Heal Your Life*.
**Hollie Holden** and **Robert Holden** PhD, author of *Life Loves You, Loveability* and *Shift Happens*

One of the greatest gifts we can give ourselves is the gift of self-love. Yet often our early life experiences, including as Sharon points out in the book, those that took place in the womb and at birth, teach us to be self-critical and even self-loathing. In *Heal Your Birth, Heal Your Life*, Sharon shows us how to go to the earliest moments in life when we learned to be less loving towards ourselves, believing we were undeserving of love, and how to rewrite them. This equates to more self-love and compassion for ourselves in the present.
**David R Hamilton** PhD, author of *I ♥ Me: The Science of Self-Love, How Your Mind Can Heal Your Body* and *Why Kindness is Good for You*

This book has been half a decade in the making. I first encountered Sharon King's work on Matrix Birth Reimprinting over five years ago when I was co-authoring the Matrix Reimprinting book with the creator of the technique, Karl Dawson.

Sharon's work is remarkable in every way. She helped me heal my own birth story, and has helped countless other people around the world do the same. When I was involved in Matrix Reimprinting, I shared Sharon's work with people around the world and was always amazed at the difference that a Matrix Birth Reimprinting session could make to someone's life. I often saw radical transformations in one-hour sessions.

I have been waiting for Sharon to bring this book out since then, and I know that it will make a profound impact on the birth trauma scene. What is unique about this book is not just the groundbreaking technique that Sharon has developed, but the way she grounds it in a plethora of scientific, and other research.

Whether you are a practitioner wanting to develop your skills, someone who has experienced a birth trauma, or you are about to give birth and want to make sure you create the best environment possible for your baby, this book is a groundbreaking resource that will ensure deep and lasting transformation in your own life, and the lives of those around you.

**Sasha Allenby**, co-author of *Matrix Reimprinting Using EFT*. Author of *Write an Evolutionary Self-Help Book – The Definitive Guide for Spiritual Entrepreneurs*

This is a significant book and an excellent method to help people access and heal the often unrecognised and earliest origins of many of their lifelong emotional and physical problems.

**Phyllis Klaus**, MFT, LMSW, co-author of *Bonding*, *The Doula Book*, *Your Amazing Newborn*, and *When Survivors Give Birth*

Sharon King's work has transformed my life. Not only for my own birth story, but it has created vital breakthroughs in my work with clients. So much so, I trained with her in Matrix Birth Reimprinting. Sharon's book *Heal Your Birth, Heal Your Life* is well researched and is full of page-turning 'Ahas', that make so much sense. I'm not sure if Sharon has written a book or started a revolution in holistic birthing!

**Becky Walsh**, author of *You Do Know*

Sharon King has written a succinct blending of science and practical wisdom for parents, parents-to-be, practitioners, and all of us who were once babies. Stories are woven throughout to make this very readable and the work very do-able. You'll have an understanding of your own early story and how that may be impacting you in present time, as well as the tools to help you release those things that no longer serve you. In my own experience, working in the matrix with Sharon is a powerful process and can literally change everything. As the title says: Heal Your Birth, Heal Your Life. Couldn't have said it better. Bravo! This is a must-read book!

**Rebecca Thompson**, author of *Consciously Parenting: What it Really Takes to Raise Emotionally Healthy Families*


Having experienced the flowing, non-linear process of Matrix Birth Reimprinting at the hands (and heart) of this gifted healer, I wondered how it could ever be captured in a book – but Sharon King has done it! In *Heal Your Birth, Heal Your Life*, not only has she offered us a clear explanation of this powerful healing modality and its theoretical foundations, but she has embedded it in a clear context of prenatal psychology. A few of the more technical chapters may speak more to practitioners, but most will speak to all those who seek to understand how their lives have been (and continue to be!) shaped by their own births and/or the births of their children. And more importantly, this book speaks to those who seek to grow beyond imprinted patterns of limitation and fear.

**Marcy Axness**, PhD, author of *Parenting for Peace: Raising the Next Generation of Peacemakers*


*Heal Your Birth, Heal Your Life* by Sharon King is a book whose time has come. The title of this book alone may cause many to query its meaning. Great! Having been in the field for over 35 years I can say that this book is 'what it says on the tin'.

Perhaps our most important and significant healing is that which comes from healing our source experience – our original trauma in life – and the decisions we made about it. Since we build our perceptions of our life on each previous experience, the net result is a compounding of these events, which can have a multiplier effect. As such, the tools developed and presented by Ms King are important, and even crucial, to a happy and fulfilling life experience. Highly recommended.

**Patrick Houser**, author of *Fathers-To-Be Handbook*

Beliefs formed at our birth can impact us for a lifetime. In *Heal Your Birth, Heal Your Life*, Sharon shares her vast experience helping people to heal the highly impactful experiences that often occur at the life-defining moments around their birth. This is an important book that ultimately proves it is never too late to be born free and have a truly fulfilling life.

**Sandy Newbigging**, author of *Mind Calm* and *Body Calm*

There are emotional booby traps – trigger points hidden in everyone's body. Come close and unconscious anxiety and fears explode. We feel them but don't realise that these ghosts are from our prenatal experience, birth and very early experiences. Becoming aware of these emotional booby traps is one thing. Releasing the ghosts is another. What seemed so esoteric a few years ago – that your birth and very early experiences are alive and very expressive – today is no longer a secret. Love, acceptance, forgiveness and focused attention transforms – now! Sharon King, in *Heal Your Birth, Heal Your Life*, shares powerful tools to do just that.

**Michael Mendizza**, founder of Touch the Future

Having just read *Heal Your Birth, Heal Your Life*, I must say I was completely blown away! It is an absolutely brilliant book. Beautifully written in an easy-to-understand way, Sharon educates us about how our birth experiences can shape our whole life. She eloquently talks about the effects the different birthing processes have on us and how they can cause trauma to the baby, the mother and the father. Not only does she talk about the effects, but also offers practical information on how we can release these traumas and change the harmful beliefs that were created during that time. Everyone should read this book! Practitioners will learn many useful resources to use with their clients; lay people will learn how to heal their traumas and change beliefs that have affected their lives negatively; medical and health professionals will understand how their interventions affect the baby; and pretty much everyone can take something positive from this book. It's not just for pregnant women or new parents: this book is useful for everyone who has ever been born!

**Vera Malbaski**, EFT and Matrix Reimprinting Trainer

# Heal YOUR BIRTH Heal YOUR LIFE

## SHARON KING

Foreword by Karl Dawson

**SilverWood**

Published in 2015 by SilverWood Books

SilverWood Books Ltd
14 Small Street, Bristol, BS1 1DE, United Kingdom
www.silverwoodbooks.co.uk

ISBN 978-1-78132-374-8 (paperback)
ISBN 978-1-78132-375-5 (ebook)

British Library Cataloguing in Publication Data
A CIP catalogue record for this book is available from the British Library

Set in Myriad Pro by SilverWood Books
Printed on responsibly sourced paper

While Matrix Reimprinting, Matrix Birth Reimprinting and EFT have produced
remarkable clinical results, they must still be considered to be in the experimental
stage and thus practitioners and the public must take complete responsibility for
their use of these techniques. Furthermore, Sharon King is not a licensed health
professional and offers Matrix Reimprinting, Matrix Birth Reimprinting and EFT
as a personal performance coach and holistic therapist.

This book is intended for information purposes only and is not intended to be
a substitute for medical advice. The author does not dispense medical advice or
prescribe the use of any technique as a form of treatment for physical or medical
problems without the advice of a physician, either directly or indirectly. Always
consult a qualified medical practitioner. Any use of information in this book is at the
reader's discretion and risk. Neither the author nor the publisher can be held
responsible for any loss, claim or damage arising out of the use, or misuse, of the
suggestions made, the failure to take medical advice or for any material
on third party websites.

Many of the names in the case studies have been changed to protect the identity
of the individuals in question.

*This book is dedicated to my mother and father
and to all the mothers and fathers in the world.
Without you, we would not be who we are meant to be.*

*Despite our entrance into the world, or even because of it, we become the
magical people we are. Each and every one of us has a story to tell about
birth, life and death.*

*Now is the time to tell and transform our stories.*

**Sharon King**

# Contents

# Acknowledgements

*Every book has a whole team that contributes towards bringing it into physical form: I thank you all.* **Sharon King**

My book, *Heal Your Birth, Heal Your Life*, has come about because of experiences with many brave and courageous people. There are those who have become leaders in their chosen field of excellence and who have taught me the basics of my craft; there are those who are clients and friends who have chosen to heal the traumas from their past, and who have helped me develop and refine the Matrix Birth Reimprinting techniques.

My first massive thank you goes to Karl Dawson, my mentor, guide, teacher and friend. He is the man who not only changed my life beyond all recognition but who is also the agent of change for everyone he meets. Little did I consciously know that my first weekend in Findhorn learning EFT in April 2007 was going to change the course of my life and begin the most amazing journey for me. Karl, you described me as being like a "deer caught in the headlights" that weekend – maybe my subconscious already knew what was about to unfold for me and got a little frightened. I have immense gratitude and love for you, as you have always listened, guided, encouraged and pushed me firmly out into the world to spread my wings and fly.

I also thank Ted Wilmont: you took me under your wing in the early days of being a practitioner and ever so patiently answered all of my hundreds of questions and gave me confidence to go on a deeper journey with my clients and continue my own healing journey.

Sasha Allenby: thank you, my friend and birthing partner. Without you this book would have never made it into physical form. With your brilliant creative ability you have made what felt like the hardest task in the world be the most joyful and easiest. Working with you on birthing this book and following your Write Your Book In 12 Weeks program has been a key contributing factor to getting this book written, finished and published.

To my editor, Lois Rose: every book needs a midwife and you have lovingly crafted this book into shape and guided both it and me safely on to the last part of our birthing journey.

To Helen Hart and all the team at SilverWood Books: you have taken the fear out of publishing this book and made me feel supported and loved. Thank you. To my friends Lyra Crawford and Vera Malbaski: you both did a wonderful job proofreading the book.

Ryan Dana from the HeartMath Institute: thank you from the bottom of my heart for your endless patience and support.

A big thank you to each and every client I have worked with: you have helped me learn and grow.

There have been some key clients who have contributed most to the development of the Matrix Birth Reimprinting technique and I would like to honour these clients individually.

Caroline, without you, I may never have discovered Matrix Birth Reimprinting. Thank you for being the first wonderful mother I worked with, who had the desire to find another way to birth a baby naturally without fear. The first session we experienced clearing the trauma of the birth of your two boys, your own birth experience and the future birth of baby Archie is now the foundation of my work. I am so delighted to hear that you have gone on to have another baby and had another totally natural birth. (You can read Caroline's story in Chapter 1.)

Josephine and George: your sessions to clear the trauma of the loss of your two special baby boys awakened a passion in me to help others to heal from such tragic losses and to teach others to do the same.

Meggie and Jake: your sessions were the first to help me realise that we can work surrogately to help transform physical illness for our children. How exciting is that!

To my friends and mentors in the birthing world in America: I would also like to say a massive thank you to you.

Suzanne Arms, you are a beautiful, generous, open-hearted woman. You took me under your wing and introduced me to other awesome friends, such as Rebecca Thompson from the Consciously Parenting Group, Dr Marcy Axness, author of *Parenting for Peace*, and Patrick Houser, author of *Fathers-To-Be Handbook*. Thank you, each and every one of you, for openly sharing your knowledge, support and your friendship. I am truly honoured to be working alongside you all.

Susie Shelmerdine, my soul sister: I am so grateful that we are walking very similar paths in life together. Thank you for your continued support, your love and non-judgement – they mean the world to me.

To my other teachers and friends: Melissie Jolly, creator of the Colour Mirrors system and author of *What the Seeker Found*: your deep wisdom always astounds me. You have taught me so much.

Sandy Newbigging, creator of Mind Calm meditation: thank you for teaching me to open to conscious awareness and helping me to finally find peace in my life.

Becky Walsh, author of *You Do Know: Learning to Act on Intuition Instantly*: thank you for coming into my life at the right time to help support me in getting the message of this book out into the world.

And finally to my other friends: Brett Moran, Sami Thorpe, Korani, Maria Madden, Mel Grout and Celia Castle, who have lovingly held the space for me to freak out whilst writing this book and are still speaking to me: thank you.

Oh, and I nearly forgot my beautiful horse, Charlie, who willingly (well, most of the time), carries me around through the woods and listens to my thoughts and helps me get clear about life, the universe and everything.

I love you all.

# Foreword by Karl Dawson

I first encountered Sharon King almost a decade ago. I created a technique called Matrix Reimprinting, which has become an internationally recognised tool for dealing with trauma. I co-authored two books on the subject, which were published by industry leaders Hay House. The first book is currently in ten languages.

I met Sharon before Matrix Reimprinting had reached the worldwide stage. In fact, it was in its early development stages. A number of people around me were there for the pivotal stage of developing the technique – sharing the experiences they had while using it with clients, adding ideas and shaping concepts. Sharon was one of those.

As Matrix Reimprinting became stronger, several of the people in my circle started to develop their own specialities with it. One of those was Sharon. She had a passion for what was taking place in the womb and around birth, and how this was impacting our later lives. She extensively researched and studied in a whole host of other fields to bring together her understanding of birth trauma and how it can be healed.

One of the main principles of Matrix Reimprinting is that our beliefs are formed in the first six years, when we are in a highly programmable state. These beliefs become the framework through which we operate. This is also the topic of my second book, *Transform Your Beliefs, Transform Your Life*. I am passionate about the subject of beliefs as I have seen how healing them can transform our physical, emotional and mental wellbeing, and totally change how we show up in the world.

Stanford professor and cell biologist Bruce Lipton shows how our beliefs, as well as the environments that we are raised in, affect our biology. Matrix Reimprinting can take us back to key moments in our life when our beliefs were formed – when environmental influences and other key traumas changed the way we see the world. With the tool I created, we can literally rewrite what we learned on that day. When the beliefs are rewritten, the body and the emotions transform accordingly, as does our outlook on life.

Sharon has taken her vast knowledge and understanding into an important area of human life, by highlighting how many of these beliefs are formed in the womb and at birth. She has a whole system of working with transforming beliefs, which enables us to go back to when we were in the womb and when we were born. How we come into the world matters. The old paradigm belief that babies do not have any conscious awareness or feel any physical pain has been proven to be antiquated. Our modern birthing systems have a lot to answer for in terms of trauma. And when the baby comes into the world and learns that it is not a safe place, because of the trauma they experience, this can shape the way they see the world from that day forward.

As well as our Western birthing systems, there are the beliefs that we learn from our families. And we are often born into families who have emotional challenges. These can impact us in the womb too. Sharon's work can help pinpoint these challenges and change them. This in turn affects the filters of our perception in the current day.

This work is based on Matrix Reimprinting but has some aspects that are unique to Matrix Birth Reimprinting. One of those is the process of reimprinting the birth. If you experienced a traumatic birth or were not effectively bonded with your mother (which can cause all kinds of attachment issues later in life), you can release your birth trauma and then rewrite your birth in the way you would have liked it to be. This is a profound experience, and for many it has been life-changing.

I've seen some outstanding results with the Matrix Birth Reimprinting work. Mothers who had experienced several highly traumatic births, and were about to give birth again, changed the way their next birth unfolded by clearing the trauma of the past. I've even seen mothers who clear up the issues that they had giving birth, and the health or wellbeing of their child changes accordingly.

This is remarkable work that has been tried and tested all over the world. It is for lay people who want to rewrite their birth trauma, or want to ensure that when they give birth, it is without any of the trauma of the past. But it is also for practitioners who want to help their clients on a really deep level. This is a classic book for Matrix Reimprinting – well researched and well written. I am delighted and proud to count it among the books for Matrix Reimprinting.

**Karl Dawson**
Creator of Matrix Reimprinting

# Introduction

Often, when a new transformational tool or technique is created, you will hear the originator say that they stumbled upon it by accident. Although there are elements of accidental creation in the Matrix Birth Reimprinting protocol, I would say that it was very much like a planned birth! That is, the foundations and research that I had laid down on the run up to it coming forward were very much part of the creation that followed.

At the time that this method came to me, I was quite far along my own personal and professional journey with EFT – a meridian energy technique that involves tapping on various acupuncture points while verbalising a specific statement about an issue or challenge you are facing. The technique, which we will explore for your personal use later in this book, is used globally by millions to resolve both physical and emotional challenges. I was also very closely involved in the development of Matrix Reimprinting – an advanced EFT technique created by Karl Dawson, which has gone on to become a worldwide phenomenon. Matrix Reimprinting is an advanced EFT technique that involves going back to any life trauma we may have experienced, that shaped our sense of self, our beliefs and our identity, and literally rewriting it. Matrix Reimprinting is based on the principle of quantum physics, i.e. that we are all connected by a unified energy field, known as the matrix. Our most challenging life experiences are held as pictures in the matrix in the form of Energetic Consciousness Holograms or ECHOs. With Matrix Reimprinting we can interact with these ECHOs held in our fields (or in other words, the matrix) to transform these past pictures. Many of our early life experiences create imprints that we continue to tune into on a subconscious level. These experiences shape the way we see ourselves and the way we show up in the world. By rewriting them, along with the accompanying beliefs that were created in those moments, our perception of ourselves, and our world, transforms accordingly.

I have worked with thousands of clients all over the world using these techniques to resolve traumatic memories – everything from sexual trauma, to war trauma, to family trauma, to natural disasters – and seen miracles every day using Matrix Reimprinting. Clients who believed they were scarred for life and who had given up all hope of a 'normal' reality, rewrote the traumatic memories, released the trauma from their systems, and healed, both physically and emotionally.

It was a great honour to be part of the development of Matrix Reimprinting and watch it develop into a worldwide phenomenon. And as this groundbreaking technique began to shape the way that tens of thousands of people resolved trauma, I started to hear my own calling. One of the key components of Matrix Reimprinting is the work of cell biologist Bruce Lipton, who correlates the connection between beliefs and biology. Dr Lipton's work and research literally show how beliefs influence biology, and subsequently turn on and off the expression of certain genes. This affects our health and wellbeing, and our susceptibility to disease. One factor, crucial to this work, is that Dr Lipton shows how these beliefs are formed both in the womb, and in the first six years of childhood (something that we will explore in greater detail later in this book). Much of Karl Dawson's work with Matrix Reimprinting enables us to go back to the first six years of life when beliefs were formed. But at this stage, we weren't focusing so much on what happened in the womb.

Simultaneously, I began to develop a fascination with the way that babies are birthed in the Western world. If beliefs were formed when babies were in utero and in the first six years, then what, exactly, was happening when their first encounter with the world was a harsh, clinical jolt into reality? I learnt from Body Talk, another technique I was studying at the time, that a baby can either withdraw or develop its senses at the time of birth. In America, for example, silver nitrate drops are put into the baby's eyes just in case the mother has a sexually transmitted disease. Aside from the data that correlates this practice with the wearing of glasses early on in life, I began to ask myself what kind of shock this was creating for the baby, especially given that silver nitrate creates a harsh, stinging sensation and more importantly, blurs the vision, hindering the bonding process.[1]

Right there in that moment, potentially there is the belief being formed for each child that goes through this procedure that it is not safe to see or look out on the world. As we go through this book we will explore more about how these beliefs are formed and how they influence our lives. At this stage, I was just beginning to realise the impact that our standard Western birthing process, including blood tests, suctioning and other harsh medical procedures, was having on shaping the beliefs of babies as they came into the world.

Throughout this book, I will share with you some revealing truths about the impact that these procedures have on our beliefs, our physical being, and our perception of self. But most importantly, I will be introducing a brand-new technique – one that I created – that can radically transform your relationship to your birth.

I will introduce Matrix Birth Reimprinting and how it came about in Chapter 1. What follows in this book is what I uncovered in the five years after that first session and how, despite never having given birth myself, I earned myself the nickname of 'Mamma King' after reimprinting literally thousands of women (and a number of men) worldwide.

Whether you experienced a traumatic birth when you came into the world, whether you gave birth previously and it was challenging, or you are about to give birth and want to make sure it goes as smoothly as possible, what is contained within these pages will enable you to clear any subconscious blocks you have to a free and easy birth and to reimprint both your past and your future.

And now, I will share with you how Matrix Birth Reimprinting came about.

# Part 1

# Introducing the Tools

# Chapter 1

# How Matrix Birth Reimprinting Came About

*Whenever and however you give birth, your experience will impact your emotions, your mind, your body, and your spirit for the rest of your life.*
**Ina May Gaskin**

Caroline showed up in my life when she was five months pregnant with her third child. She was also racked with fear about giving birth. When I asked her to explain the nature of her fear, considering that she had given birth to two boys before, she told me how both her previous birth experiences had been highly traumatic. She was convinced that the third one was going to be the same. She explained how both boys had been very long, intensive labours, with medical intervention, and finally when she had given birth, she experienced a lot of trouble breastfeeding, something she had set her heart on doing.

I learnt that when Caroline became pregnant with her second baby, she had been told that no two births were ever the same, and that the second birth would be different. When this turned out not to be the case for her, it created two beliefs for Caroline, the first one being that you can't trust what the doctors tell you and the second one being that this next birth was likely to be equally traumatic. At this stage, the fear was all-consuming for her.

Using both the EFT tapping technique and Matrix Reimprinting (two techniques that I will introduce you to in later chapters), we explored her first birth. With Matrix Reimprinting it is as if you are going back in time to remember what you experienced and felt about life on that day, so that you can change it. When we went back to the first birth, Caroline could literally see herself lying on the bed in the hospital, strapped up to the heart monitor. The thing that stood out for her was the sound of the baby's heartbeat on the monitor. She remembered that she could hear it dipping in and out, and the more stressed she got, the more her unborn child seemed to be responding with stress of his own.

We used Matrix Reimprinting to release the stress for both herself, and her unborn child. The interesting thing about this technique is that once you release the stress from the memory, it often changes how you remember it. Once the fear was cleared, Caroline could then hear her baby's heart beating more consistently on the monitor.

"That's really amazing," she said, with tears in her eyes. We actually recreated the new 'memory' further, so that there were sounds of waves gently lapping on a beach and she could see herself and her unborn baby relaxing.

It's important to note that rewriting these pictures is having an effect on a subconscious level. It isn't that we are denying what actually happened. Instead, we are rewriting the subconscious information that is telling us the world is not safe. The subconscious stores traumatic memories for future moments in an attempt to try to protect us from something similar happening to us again. It isn't working against us. However, sometimes what it stores is not useful to us. In the case of Caroline, it was storing the old memory of the heart monitor from her first birth, and creating a similar stress for any subsequent births. By rewriting this memory, we were letting Caroline's subconscious know that it was now safe to give birth without fear.

There were still further elements of this birthing experience that needed to be rewritten. The next traumatic moment of this first birth was when the midwife was really pushing for her to have an epidural, although Caroline was set against it. She protested, but then finally gave in and agreed. However, it took two hours from when she agreed, to when the epidural was administered. The midwife hadn't checked Caroline during this time, and just after it was administered, Caroline learnt that she could have given birth naturally after all, as she was at that point almost fully dilated. She was utterly devastated by the flippancy of the midwife, as she had been so determined to have a natural birth. After I helped her to release the resentment towards the midwife using tapping and the Matrix Reimprinting protocol, Caroline was able to see that the midwife was doing the best with the knowledge and experience she had at that time. She also chose to rewrite the memory with an angelic figure, whom she named Annie, as the midwife. The new memory included a natural, unmedicated birth at home, bonding with her first baby, Luke, and breastfeeding him in her living room.

What came next was the surprising part. (At least, at the time it was surprising. From the thousands of Matrix Birth Reimprinting sessions I have done since then, it now seems normal to me!) When I asked Caroline where we needed to go next, she replied that she needed to look at her own birth.

When she went back in time to when she was born, Caroline was surprised to find that her own mother had experienced a similar fear to the one that had occurred with the birth of Luke. Sometimes things are picked up on a subconscious level that we don't know on a conscious level when we do this work, and that is what happened to Caroline. What we will also explore as we go through this book is how issues can create energetic fields which then become repeated down the generations. I used the EFT tapping protocol and Matrix Reimprinting with Caroline to clear these generational fields and the accompanying stress that went with them (and I will teach you how to do this for yourself later).

The challenge also went deeper. Caroline revealed that when she was born, she had yellow jaundice and she had to stay in hospital for 2 weeks. For some of this time, Caroline had been left in the hospital alone, which had created abandonment issues. We subsequently released these for Caroline's younger self, and gave her a sense of security and wellbeing with the reimprinting process. Again, the angelic figure Annie was brought into the picture to give her a sense of security.

Interestingly, when we came to reimprint the birth of Caroline's second boy, Jamie, a lot of the fear of what had gone before had resolved. This is often the case when we clear the energetic field of an early event

27

using these techniques – sometimes the events that follow have lost their emotional charge.

There was one element of Jamie's birth that required attention, though. Just as he was being born, the midwife twisted his head to get him out, which had left him with a neck problem. We reimprinted the memory, widening the womb so he could get out a little easier. Then once again the familiar angelic figure, Annie, was brought into the scene, taking over the role of midwife, and we finished with a picture of Caroline breastfeeding and bonding with Jamie.

At this stage Caroline and I were both in awe of the experience we had just shared. We had no idea how long we had been working on these events, as time seems to warp when you are doing work of this nature. According to the clock, it was two hours, but on many levels it felt like five minutes. I got one further hit of intuition as I looked at her belly, swollen with five months of pregnancy.

"How about if we finish off by just showing your baby how the birth is going to be in the future?" I asked.

"Yes! That would be amazing," she replied.

Caroline connected to her unborn baby by placing her hands on her belly, and letting him know that the fear she had been feeling was now gone. She told him: "You are safe, and I love you."

She also told me that she was feeling emotional because on the drive over, without even knowing that we were going to do this session today, she'd actually set up in her mind where she wanted to give birth and who she wanted to be there. We recreated this room in her mind's eye, with the angelic figure Annie now also present, alongside her husband. She brought her two boys, Jamie and Luke, into the picture too. She then guided herself through the future birthing process to show her baby how the birth was going to be. We imprinted this picture, with Caroline bonding with him and breastfeeding easily.

After the session, Caroline and I were completely high! We knew that something incredibly special had taken place. I sensed immediately that this was the birth of something bigger than Caroline's personal experience.

However, for Caroline, the results were almost instantaneous. Her husband instantly noticed a difference in her. She was much more relaxed, her fear of giving birth had dissipated, and she was generally happier. People who knew the boys also began commenting on how they seemed much lighter, and how much closer and happier the whole family unit was. The changes were subtle but perceptible. Another benefit was that when Caroline's husband worked away, she felt different. In the past when he was away, her abandonment issues, dating from those early days alone in the hospital, would be triggered. These had resolved, along with her sense of separation in the world.

But the most incredible aspect of this experience was the birth of her new baby, Archie.

It turned out that the actual birth itself was relatively quick and painless. She said, "He came out easily, just as we had envisioned, and we connected and bonded straight away. I breastfed almost instantly – in fact, it was just like what it was in that picture we created. That was *exactly* how the birth was!"

The other thing that she said she noticed was that two hours after giving birth, she left her room to go to the bathroom, and observed how the other women walking down the corridor who had given birth a few days before were holding onto the walls, and walking as though they had been horse riding for a solid week! It was at this point that she noticed just how good her body was feeling. She actually didn't feel like she had just given birth. She was a little bit sore, but that was all.

I realised I was onto something. This method that I had stumbled upon was a technique in its own right. And it had the potential to be life changing too.

The next stage, which we will explore in Chapter Two, is the understanding that, contrary to popular belief, babies *are* conscious beings.

# Chapter 2

# Consciousness of the Baby

*The truth is, much of what we have traditionally believed about babies is false. We have misunderstood and underestimated their abilities. They are not simple beings but complex and ageless – small creatures with unexpectedly large thoughts.* **David Chamberlain, PhD**

In recent years there was a video clip on social media about a doctor who sang to babies as he delivered them. Having delivered over 8,000 babies, Dr Carey Andrew-Jaja claimed to have sung to most of them. The video became a viral sensation with over a million hits on YouTube.

The reason this was such an anomaly is because it is such a far cry from the delivery room of a standard Western hospital. While the singing doctor obviously had some kind of understanding of the importance of the way babies arrive into the world, the majority of the doctors in the West essentially share the belief that babies are not aware and that they feel no pain – or if they do feel pain they will not remember it.

In the same way that scientists initially conducted animal experiments with the belief that the animals could feel nothing, so a large majority of doctors still operate under this assumption, giving injections, sticking sharp objects into the baby's foot (known as heel prick blood test), squirting chemical formulas in their eyes, even holding them upside down and smacking them to make them cry. This is not just a Western phenomenon either. In some countries, circumcisions are actually performed in the absence of any pain relief.

What we are going to explore through this chapter, and continue to touch upon frequently in this book, is that babies not only experience pain (they feel it up to four times more acutely than adults[2]), but that they are, indeed, aware, both in the womb and when they are born.

Babies have what is known as implicit memory, i.e. a memory that is not within consciousness. We could also refer to implicit memory as subconscious memory. Although as adults we may not recall what occurs in the womb and at birth as a series of conscious memories, we do have a felt sense that can be accessed as a body feeling. That body feeling becomes part of our conditioning and programming as a human being. When newborns are handled as though they don't feel pain, an imprint is created: an underlying feeling that the world in which they've arrived is not safe or OK. And it is an imprint that can set the tone for the creation of a host of fear-based beliefs throughout life.

Our body-minds are very much like computers, downloading information from our external reality and shaping our perceptions and our world from the information we gathered. You can download any number of programmes to your hard drive. Some that you accumulate are very useful. Others are obsolete, just sitting there and taking up space. Others are damaging to the system.

It's pretty much the same when it comes to the way we are wired as humans. It begins at conception. Even though it is unlikely that you remember the details of your conception, imprints were being formed, even then. They were being formed the whole time you were in the womb. And they continued to be formed in the delivery room and beyond.

Just in case this is triggering something in you, particularly if you are currently pregnant or a new parent and wondering if you have created similar imprints for your baby, throughout this book we are also going to explore how these imprints can be rewritten, and how you can actually do this on your baby's behalf. Say, for example, you were shocked when you found out you were pregnant. If this is the case, maybe you went so far as to think that you might terminate the pregnancy. We can use the Matrix Birth Reimprinting process in an incident such as this to go back to that moment and release the shock that you were feeling. We can even let your baby know that it wasn't personal, and that it was only about what was going on with you at that time. Even though a baby feels it on an energetic level and they can feel as though it is personal (we'll explore this more later), we can enable them to release this feeling and help them see that it wasn't the case, however much time has passed.

Sometimes when we do a Reimprinting session such as the above, especially if it is an adult going back to a similar experience and 'remembering' it (which happens more frequently than you might think with the tools I am sharing with you in this book), there can be a lot of rage and fear. It is a survival mechanism that has been triggered within them, and their reaction is a fear-based emotional response. The tools that are presented in this book can help them release this fear.

Interestingly, although I have worked with almost every conception and birthing issue that you could possibly imagine, the one scenario I haven't worked with yet is that of an IVF, or test-tube, baby. I would be fascinated to see what this created, as I imagine a child conceived in this way may have its own set of beliefs or imprints to deal with. If you or your baby were conceived in a test tube, you can still use these techniques to get to the heart of any belief this may have created for you.

A mother's reaction to pregnancy is just one of the things that a foetus can feel. There are a host of other imprints that impact the unborn baby. These include the father's reaction, any physical or emotional trauma that the mother experienced during pregnancy, anything such as deaths or losses in the family, arguments or feuds that the mother is involved in, and so on, and we will explore these more, throughout this chapter.

## Life Lessons

I also want to reiterate that there is no blame or judgement when we talk about the life challenges that may have contributed to a baby's experience. I have a wider belief, which is that we come into this world to learn certain lessons. My overall sense is that we choose certain experiences in this lifetime so we can learn and grow. Even if you don't share this belief, I still want to invite you to come from a place of non-judgement with this work. The majority of people in this world are not consciously wanting to create trauma for another human being. Doctors, midwives, our parents, our partners, we ourselves – are all doing the best we can with the knowledge and understanding we have in any given moment. People who do consciously cause pain to another are coming from a place of pain themselves. We all have our own stories gathered from our past experiences and beliefs. As you and I go on this journey together, think of us as scientists working to unravel the imprints of the past. We are merely uncovering any programming that has been created and then rewriting it with the tools that follow in a practical manner. Of course, there may be emotions involved, and we have tools to deal with those too. But essentially, our job is to uncover and rewrite what took place in the past, so that peace can be experienced in the present.

## What Do We Mean by Consciousness?

We have been talking about the consciousness of the baby, so I want to clarify what I mean by that. Chances are, if you are reading this book, it's not the first time you have been exposed to the idea that we are spiritual beings in a physical body. Whether you are new to this concept or it is a familiar one to you, I want to take a moment to distinguish between your consciousness and your filters.

Most of us have been conditioned to experience life through our filters. It is as though there are two versions of what is happening – the actual event that is taking place and the story we are projecting onto it. Our conditioned responses to our external world shape how we perceive our reality.

Beyond the story of who you are and what happened to you in this lifetime, there is your conscious awareness. This is the part of you that can observe all your thoughts and feelings. Even though you have most likely been entrained into believing that your thoughts and feelings *are* who you are, and you have been taught to react to them accordingly, your conscious awareness exists independently of what happened to you and how you feel about it.

If this idea is new to you, try this really simple exercise. Set a timer for one minute. Close your eyes. Then start counting your thoughts. See how many thoughts you have in one minute. Then ask yourself this: "Who is the one that was counting the thoughts?" The one that was counting them is your conscious awareness. It exists when there are no thoughts and also when you are having thoughts.

Similarly, your conscious awareness exists independently of your emotional state. Most of the time when you experience an emotion, you become that emotion, or at least it feels like you do. But have you ever had the experience of noticing a thought such as 'I am really angry right now'? Not outwardly expressing this in a fit of rage, but rather just observing that anger is rising in you? That is your consciousness aware of your anger.

Some spiritual or esoteric teachers describe the difference between these as your 'me' and your 'I'. Your 'me' is a collection of all the things that happened to you in this lifetime. It is a series of triggers and programmes that form your perception of yourself. Your 'I' is the eternal self that exists beyond the triggers and programmes.

Usually our 'me' takes centre stage. In spiritual awakening, we have what spiritual teacher Adyashanti calls 'a change of occupancy', where the 'me' is no longer at the centre of everything, and you experience life through the 'I' of conscious awareness.

Children operate through a slightly different kind of conscious awareness. They are experiencing life as they see it, but they aren't aware that they are doing so.

In Chapter 12, we will explore how they are like sponges, absorbing the world around them as if it were the truth. The more they are exposed to threatening situations, the more they start to live through their filters.

If you have ever had an experience of looking at a small child and feeling like they have already had a 'hard life', you will understand what I mean. Later we will talk about what happens in the brain chemistry of a child whose mother has been continuously triggered into survival. But for now, the essential thing to grasp is that babies experience consciousness. It is slightly different to what adults experience in spiritual awakening, when all the filters of conditioning are removed, although it has similar qualities (for example, when many people experience spiritual awakening they have that child-like wonder about them).

I think the simplest way to understand the consciousness of a baby is to perceive it as 'awareness'. We have generally assumed that babies aren't aware, and they are actually aware of everything. When we understand this, it changes our whole perception of the experience of childhood. And yet, on some level, you may even remember how aware you were as a child. It is this awareness that we will be working with throughout the whole of this book.

## The Womb

We have already established that babies perceive their environment and are able to recall it.

During the 1995 APPPAH (Association for Prenatal and Perinatal Psychology and Health) Congress in San Francisco, Dr David Chamberlain, PhD shared the following case, which is a typical example of the consciousness of prenates. A mother was undergoing an amniocentesis. Videotapes of the amniocentesis showed that when the needle was inserted into the uterus, the baby turned toward the needle and batted it away. Thinking that they had seen an aberration, the medical staff repeated the needle insertion, and again, the same thing happened. There are also numerous anecdotal reports that babies routinely withdraw from needles as they are inserted into the uterus. From these observations, it is safe to conclude that babies are very conscious of what is happening around them, particularly with respect to events that impact them personally[3].

Something else of importance to consider is that while babies are in the womb, they have no true sense of self, or of being separate from their mother's life experience. Everything that the mother feels, the baby records as its own. What the mother feels, the baby feels. What the mother ingests, the baby receives.

This mother-baby relationship has several aspects to it. On a physical level, the baby receives the same hormones produced by the mother from her bloodstream through the placenta. For example, during a stressful or fearful situation our cortisol levels go up and hormones such as adrenaline are released to enable us to react to the situation and take appropriate action such as running away or fighting. And if the mother is feeling loved, relaxed, supported and safe, chemicals such as oxytocin, which is known as 'the love hormone', and serotonin and dopamine, the mood-boosting, feel-good chemicals, will be produced. It is also my belief that the mother's emotional states are communicated energetically to the baby. One way this may occur is via the water that surrounds the baby. Dr Masaru Emoto, scientist and author of *Messages from Water*, demonstrated with his experiments with water that it responds to positive or negative words, pictures and sounds. When water was placed in positive environments, beautiful ice crystals were formed, and when placed in negative environments, crystals were either non-existent or were distorted. Dr Emoto also demonstrated that plants can either thrive when you speak lovingly to them, or die, if you speak words of hate.[4]

The baby's body contains 78% water and is surrounded by water in utero so this may explain how these energetic messages are transported to the baby from not only their mother, but also from their father and the environment around them.

The baby receives the communication through the water via its physical and energetic systems. We are all empathic and intuitive beings whether we realise it or not. Becky Walsh, in her book *You Do Know: Learning to Act on Intuition Instantly*, describes four ways we receive intuitive information.[5]

1  Mental intuition – we receive 'downloads' of intuitive information into the creative part of our mind
2  Somatic intuition – we feel intuition physically, meaning our body is the receiver of information
3  Emotional intuition – we pick up other people's emotions and often feel them as our own
4  Spiritual intuition – we have a sensitive awareness of other energy systems around us

We all have the ability to receive information in all the four ways mentioned above; however, I believe that through our experiences in the womb, birth and early childhood, we develop a stronger sense of one or two of these ways of receiving information.

According to Dr Bruce Lipton, it is likely that, if the mother is in a peaceful and relaxed state for the majority of the pregnancy, the baby is going to have a more developed intellect. This is because if the mother is thriving rather than in survival mode, the cortex of the baby's brain becomes more developed. A mother who is in a high fear or survival state will create the opposite conditions for development and more energy will go into creating the reptilian brain (also known as the hind brain). If the mother is living in a war zone or in a violent and abusive relationship, for example, the foetus is learning that the world outside is not a safe place, and different elements of the brain are being developed so it can adapt and survive. The foetus is learning that when it comes out into the world, it is going to need to fight and its survival mechanisms are developed in a way that is going to enable its protection. Its body as well will show this learning: muscle development will be enhanced because once out in the world, fighting or running away will be necessary to survive.

There are other instances where physical conditions can develop as a result of the emotional experiences of the mother.

For example, if the mother is unsure if she wants the baby (perhaps she experienced an event that caused her to feel separate and alone during pregnancy, or she was separated from her baby at birth), then there is a possibility the baby will develop eczema. In my experience, eczema is often linked to separation. (We will explore separation further in Chapter 9.)

If the mother is living in a high state of worry, then the child is likely to be more of a worrier. It's likely to be an anxious child, growing into an anxious adult. This is simply because the baby has learnt that worry is the state it needs to be in to survive in the world and it becomes the normal default setting of their emotional state. Children born to a mother who is highly anxious may also be prone to stomach and intestinal issues, such as irritable bowel syndrome or Crohn's Disease, and have many food intolerances.

We touched on abandonment earlier, but just to reiterate, if the baby doesn't feel wanted, they are likely to have abandonment issues throughout life. They will grow into an adult who creates one abandonment after another, recreating a similar energy to that which they experienced in the womb.

Any shock in the womb also creates an imprint for the baby. This could be anything from a car accident that the mother experiences, to her seeing something shocking on the news. Generally speaking, when it's just a one-off event that's not highly traumatic, it doesn't leave too much of an imprint. In fact, small and traumatic shocks help the baby to develop resilience, so it isn't as though a mother needs to lead a sheltered life whilst she is pregnant. It is when an incident is repeated over and over again, or when it is severely traumatic, that it affects the baby's consciousness and sense of self.

## Conscious at Birth?

The following case study was taken from Dr David Chamberlain's book, *The Mind of Your Newborn Baby*. This book charts his celebrated work as a hypnotherapist regressing adults back to the womb and birth.

**Stewart**

I'm stuck! I can't move my shoulders. The doctor is pulling my head.

My jaws hurt; he's squeezing them, pulling them. Oh, my mouth! He's pulling them harder and harder, the pulling is hurting more and more…

It hurts, hurts…I feel so tight around my shoulders and the doctor is pulling and I can't get out!

He's yelling at me and pulling. "Push!" he's yelling… "Push! Push!"

Things are becoming numb.

He's pulling on my right shoulder trying to get my arm out. He's using his hands and just kind of grabbing to pull me out.

I feel that numbness all over. I feel like my bones are going to break, it's so tight!

The opening is as big as it will go and my mom's crying and pushing. She's not relaxed at all. She's tight and I'm tight and the doctor is really becoming angry because I'm not coming out like I'm supposed to.

And he's pulling at my right shoulder harder and harder. I feel caught! Then he pulls on my head. He grabs me around the jaw and the back of my neck and pulls me back and forth, kind of wiggling, pulling one side and then the other trying to get one shoulder out first.

He's trying to hurry. He says I need to breathe soon. I guess that's why he's pulling so hard on my head and right arm. He's rough!

His words are coarse, not gentle at all. He's frustrated because I'm not dropping and I'm not responding; I'm not being a normal child, not doing what I'm supposed to do.

I'm not sure what I'm supposed to do!

He says, "Mrs E, you have a stubborn child; he's not being quite normal like regular children. They're supposed to drop their hands, and he's not. He's hanging on and I'm trying to pull him down and he's fighting me, I don't know why…"
He's not saying very nice things about me. He says I give him trouble, I was difficult. He was saying to Mother that I was going to be a difficult kid. I'm not. I'm not going to be difficult, but he said I was.
Well, it was a silly thing he said about me, but everybody was in agreement; nobody was taking my side. I wanted to say, "No, I'm not!", but they wouldn't listen.
He called me a little fart! He said "Probably the little fart will be late for everything!" and he laughed like it was a joke. Everybody laughed…
I didn't know what was going on, but he said it was all my fault – those words are so clear!

> My desire to say something was strong but I couldn't.
> I couldn't say anything; I didn't know how. But I wanted to.
> Everybody was laughing and making me feel bad.[6]

As we go through this book, we will explore the impact that the doctor's words, or indeed any words spoken by an adult, can have on the impressionable subconscious of the child. In the story above, Stewart was told that he wasn't a normal child, that he wasn't doing what he was supposed to do, that he was going to be trouble. In addition, everyone was laughing at him, triggering the emotions of not being accepted and contributing to his negative belief system. We also note that Stewart talks about his desire to say something that he wasn't able to express. In Chapter 12 you will learn the Matrix Birth Reimprinting protocol, and if I were working with Stewart using this technique, I would wager that we would find the emotion caught in his throat where he was not able to express himself. I would also hazard a guess that he would have grown up with a lot of throat issues, which is common when there is something that we are unable to express or we feel we are not being heard.

In the DVD *What Babies Want*, Mary Jackson invites a young girl to set up her own birth story using small plastic toys. The girl's mother watches in amazement as she sets up the bed, puts her mother on the bed with the IV pole next to the bed, brings in her father and puts him on the right-hand side of her mother, and even puts slippers under the bed. She recreated the scene exactly, with no prompting from her mother.

She then placed the doll baby on top of her mother's tummy and then leapt into her mum's arms and gave her a huge hug (she was taken away at birth and so didn't get to do this part in real life). Not only did she tell her birth story, but she also recreated what she would have liked to happen, healing the birth story too. Babies ARE conscious at their birth!

We will learn dynamic tools that will heal any issues that were created in the consciousness of the baby, as we progress through the book.

In the next chapter, we will introduce Emotional Freedom Techniques, which is the first rung on the ladder to healing our birth stories.

# Chapter 3

# Introducing EFT Tapping Techniques

*When we accept ourselves as we are, we aren't 'settling' or 'keeping the problem in place'. We're showing love and compassion for ourselves – for our feelings, our situation, and our history.* **Nick Ortner**

In this chapter we are going to introduce and explore Emotional Freedom Techniques (EFT). This technique was created by Gary Craig, and has had phenomenal results in creating healing on both an emotional and physical level for people all over the world. It is also one of the two foundation techniques for the Matrix Birth Reimprinting protocol that I will be sharing with you later in this book.

The key thing to understand about EFT is that it releases the emotional charge associated with a life challenge you have experienced. When you go through something traumatic, an energetic charge is created that is stored in your system. The charge is there to protect you from any future similar event. For example, say as a child you were bitten by a dog. Each time you see a dog, you feel the same charge as if it were happening at that moment. Your system holds onto the sensory information in order to remind you, should any other similar danger present itself. The problem is, if you have had lots of experiences that have caused similar charges, you may find that your system is misfiring all over the place, increasing adrenaline and stress in the body, raising cortisol levels, and decreasing valuable hormones like DHEA (didehydroepiandrosterone).

The way that the tapping techniques work is that you tune into one of the following:

a) A memory that has an emotional charge.
b) Something that you are currently feeling in your body when you have been triggered by your external reality.

You then tap with your fingers on acupuncture points on the body, and release the energetic charge that the memory or the current trigger has created. Going back to the scenario of the dog, you can release all the stresses and traumas that being bitten created. You can focus on all the different aspects of what you saw, smelt, heard, felt and tasted (such as how menacing the dog's teeth looked to you, the feel of them piercing your flesh, the fact that it wouldn't let go), and tap on them individually. At the same time you can verbalize a specific statement about the event, which keeps your mind tuned in and focused upon what happened.

The result is that the energetic charge, which subsequently triggered an emotion such as fear, is released from the body and the mind simultaneously. This means that you no longer experience an unpleasant sensation in the body in relation to what went before. Any subsequent events will not have the same effect upon you. If we take our example of the dog, as long as you have tapped on both the original memory where you first got bitten, and any subsequent memories that you may have experienced of a similar nature, you will be able to encounter a dog without being triggered.

### More about How EFT Works

When you are in good health, energy flows freely through the meridians in your body. This has been recognised for thousands of years, and techniques such as acupuncture, acupressure, t'ai chi, shiatsu, qi gong and so on are designed to keep the energy flowing. Trauma and stress, in their many forms, create blocks in the energy system. If the energy is not moving properly, it does not reach and sustain vital organs, and can lead to disease.

The other thing to understand is that when we experience a traumatic event, our subconscious cannot tell the difference between whether it is happening now or it happened in the past. This is because the same chemical responses are triggered in either case. On a small scale, this happens frequently. If you bring to mind an embarrassing memory, what happens in your body? It is likely that you feel the embarrassment as though it is happening now.

What is also interesting is that we do not need to consciously remember a traumatic event for it to still be affecting us. The majority of people do not remember their very early years, yet all our experiences are recorded from conception, while in utero, and during our birth. (We'll explore more on how to easily access these subconscious memories in later chapters.)

## Introducing the EFT Tapping Protocol

The EFT tapping protocol is something that can be easily applied in any situation where there is emotional intensity. We'll explore the classic EFT protocol first and then I'll take you through a modified version of it so that you can start to experience it for yourself.

### Step 1 – First of all identify the feeling. What do you feel and where do you feel it?

The feeling is usually an emotion, showing up in the physical body. It can also be a physical sensation.

### Step 2 – How much is it affecting you on a scale of 1 to 10?

Next take a score out of ten. This is known as the **Subjective Unit of Distress Scale** (SUDs level for short). It determines how strong the issue is for you. One means it is hardly a problem and 10 means it is all-consuming. The SUDs level helps you see your progress with EFT because once you start tapping, it usually goes down.

### Step 3 – Determine the Set-Up Phrase

Both of the above components join together to form what is known as the set-up phrase.

'Even though I have this _____ (emotion or sensation) in my _____ (body part), I deeply love and accept myself.'

For example, "Even though I have this sinking in my stomach, I deeply love and accept myself."

## Step 4 – Create a Reminder Phrase

The set-up statement then gets shortened to create what is known as a reminder phrase. Use this following equation to create your reminder phrase:

What you feel + where you feel it = reminder phrase

For example: Sinking + stomach = 'This sinking in my stomach'

## Step 5 – Tapping on the Points

One at a time, tap on each of the following points (using the first two fingers of either hand, and on either side of the body). To begin, tap on the Karate Chop point and say the set-up statement 3 times. For the rest of the points, say the reminder phrase once for each point whilst tapping gently 7-8 times on each one:

1 *Karate Chop (KC)* – On the fleshy part of the hand below the outside of the little finger: the area that is the contact point when you make a karate chop motion
2 *Top of your head (TH)* – On the crown (with the flat of your fingers)
3 *Eyebrow (EB)* – At the start of your eyebrow
4 *Side of your eye (SE)* – There is a hollow at the side of your eye, after the end of your eyebrow
5 *Under your eye (UE)* – The bony part, about an inch below your pupil
6 *Under your nose (UN)* – Under your nose in the dent above your top lip

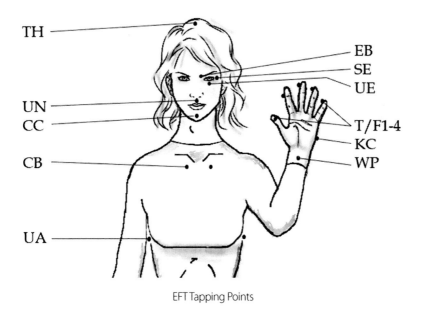

EFT Tapping Points

7  *Crease of Chin (CC)* – Under your bottom lip where the crease of your chin is

8  *On the collarbone (CB)* – Going out in a diagonal from where a gentleman's tie knot would be, you will find a hollow on either side

9  *Under the arm (UA)* – In line with the nipple for men, in line with the bra strap for women

10  *Wrist Point (WP)* – Across the inside of your wrist

11  *Thumb and finger points (T/F1-4)* – With your palm facing you, tap on the top corner of the thumbnail, and the top corner of each of the fingernails

12  *Karate Chop (KC)* – Finish where you started, on the fleshy part of the side of the hand

**Step 6 – Keep Repeating until the SUDs Level is a Zero**
Repeat several rounds of EFT until you no longer feel the original intensity of the issue you were working on.

## Learning the Tapping Technique for Yourself

The best way for you to experience the tapping technique first-hand is to use it on an emotional trigger. Without wishing to actually create a trigger for you, I want to take you through an experience of using it on yourself with something current. My question to you is this: after reading the preceding chapter, which highlighted some of the issues with the birthing methods in the West, was there anything that triggered something in you? It could have been some of the facts about the way the doctors handle babies. If you are already a parent, it might have been any fears or concerns you have about what your baby might have experienced prior to you having this knowledge. If you have given birth already and something did not go to plan, then you may be feeling sadness, guilt or anger. Or perhaps something was triggered about your own birth experience such as a feeling of fear or loneliness because you know consciously, or otherwise, that you were separated from your mother at the time of your birth. You don't necessarily need to tune into the story of what happened, just tune into the energy. Here is an overview of the tapping process.

---

**Quick Tapping Reference Guide**
The 6 steps of EFT tapping

**Step 1 – Identify the feeling**
What do you feel and where do you feel it?

**Step 2 – How much is it affecting you on a scale of 1 to 10?**
(SUDs)

**Step 3 – Determine the Set-Up Phrase**
'Even though I have this _____ (emotion or sensation) in my _____ (body part), I deeply love and accept myself.' Repeat this statement 3 times whilst tapping on the Karate chop point.

---

### Step 4 – Create a Reminder Phrase

What you feel + where you feel it = reminder phrase
Example: 'All this anger in my chest.'

### Step 5 – Tapping on the Points

Start with the top of the head and work down through the points repeating the reminder phrase.
(Refer to page 45 for a reminder of where the tapping points are.)

### Step 6 – Keep Repeating until the SUDs Level is a Zero

NB: Taking a deep breath after each round of tapping can help to relax you further and aid in the processing of the emotion.

A video of the full version of the tapping technique can be found on the membership site. Details can be found at the end of this book.

## Useful Acupressure Points
### (to use after 40 weeks of pregnancy – not during early pregnancy)

There are four acupressure points that are contraindicated during early pregnancy, but are very useful to use when the mother is over 40 weeks and she wants to stimulate her labour, turn a breech baby or aid the progress of labour. We do not generally use these as tapping points in EFT except occasionally the one above the ankle (Sp 6).

- Sp 6, which is found above the inside ankle, 4 fingers' width (1 ½") above the ankle. You will find a soft spot and it will be very sensitive. This point is used to stimulate labour. Press your finger in and out on this point. This is also a great point for menstrual cramps.
- Bl 60, found in between the anklebone and the Achilles tendon (at the back of your leg). It is used to help the baby drop down into the pelvis. Press in and out on this point.
- Bl 67 is found on the tip of the little toe and used for turning

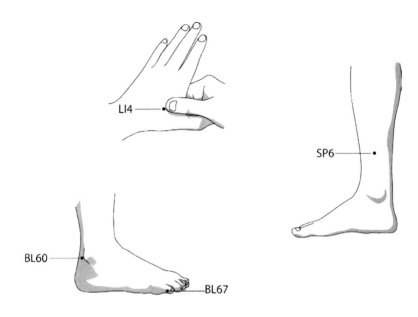

Pressure points

breech babies and stimulating labour. Pinch this point
between your fingers and hold.
• Li 4 is found on your hand between the thumb and index
finger. Pinch and hold the webbing and change hands
every 30 to 60 seconds and stop when there is a
contraction. This point encourages the delivery and eases
the process of giving birth. It is also a good point for any
pain such as headaches.[7]

## Supplemental EFT Tapping Script
## (to help you if you are triggered)

As you read though this book, there may be occasions you could be
triggered into your own experience of being born, or memories of
having given birth may be triggered. I have, for those cases, created the
following script for you to come back to at any time. I recommend you
bookmark this page.

We are not going to do the full, formal tapping protocol here, but rather give you another experience of working with the energy.

- Tap on the karate chop (KC) point on the side of your hand with the first two fingers of the opposite hand. Connect into the feeling that has come up and identify where you feel it in your body.
- What's the emotion?
- On a scale of 0-10 how high would you rate that emotion (0 being no emotion and 10 being extreme).
- If that feeling had a colour to it, what would it be?
- Does the feeling have any shape or form to it?
- Does it have any words associated with it?
- Is this feeling moving or is it static?

Having identified the energy block in your body, go through the following steps whilst tapping gently 7-8 times on each point:

Tap on your karate chop (KC) point and then keep moving around the points as you repeat the following words to yourself out loud:

KC: Even though I may not have had perfect parents, they were doing the best they could with the knowledge and understanding they had at the time, and I allow myself to find peace with this.

TH: I may not have had the perfect parents.

EB: I may not have had the perfect parents.

SE: They were doing the best that they could.

UE: They were doing the best that they could with the knowledge and understanding they had at the time.

UN: They were perfectly imperfect.

CC: They were imperfectly perfect.

CB: I allow myself to find peace with this.

UA: I allow myself to find peace with this.

WP: I allow myself to find peace.

Take a deep breath.

Back to the KC point:

(Add this round in if you are already a parent.)

KC: Even though I may not have been the perfect parent, I was doing the best I could with the knowledge and understanding that I had at that time, and I allow myself to find peace with this.

TH: I may not have been the perfect parent.

EB: I may not have been the perfect parent.

SE: I was doing the best I could.

UE: I was doing the best I could with all the knowledge and understanding I had at the time.

UN: I was also imperfectly perfect just like my parents.

CC: I was perfectly imperfect.

CB: I allow myself to find peace with this.

UA: I allow myself to find peace with this.

WP: I allow myself to find peace.

Take another deep breath.

Go back to the KC point for a third round:

KC: I may not have had the perfect birth experience, but I'm open to the possibility that I can reconnect with my parents (my child), and have the perfect birth and bonding experience for me.

TH: I may not have had the perfect birth experience.

EB: But I am open to the possibility...

SE: That I can reconnect with my parents (my child).

UE: I can reconnect.

UN: It was all perfectly imperfect.

CC: It was all imperfectly perfect.

CB: I allow myself to find peace with this.

UA: I allow myself to find peace.

WP: I allow myself to find peace.

Take another deep breath.

Take a few moments to be still, allowing the energy to settle. Now, try to access your original emotion by tuning back into your body and remembering the original trigger for you.

- How does it feel?
- What level is the emotion now from 0-10?
- Is the colour still the same or is it different?
- Is the shape or form of the energy still the same or is it different?

If you find the emotion is still at a high level, then do a few more rounds of tapping, being specific to what you are feeling and naming the emotion, colour, shape or form on each the points. Remember to take a deep breath after each full round of tapping.

If there were one point to take on board with the above exercise, it would be to remember that everything is perfectly imperfect. You and your parents *were* doing the best they could with the knowledge and wisdom available at the time. If ever you feel yourself going into judgement of yourself or of your parents, or what happened to you at your own birth, you can come back and use this tapping script.

As I mentioned in the previous chapter, my view is that everything we experience is designed to help us grow and evolve. It is my belief that, not only did we choose our birth experience, but we chose our parents as well. As I've shared earlier in this book, our birth experience sets up how we show up in life and shapes who we are (although this book will show you how to change that, should you need or want to).

The same goes for our children. If you are able to at least entertain the possibility that your child's soul chose all the experiences it has had so far, it will enable you to relax and experience more peace around the whole matter.

We have introduced EFT and you have had an experience of using it on yourself. The next chapter will explore an advanced EFT technique, Matrix Reimprinting, which you can use to understand how beliefs are formed, and transform them.

# Chapter 4

# Matrix Reimprinting and Our Belief Systems

*When you change the way you look at things, the things you look at change.* **Max Planck**

### Forming and Rewriting Limiting Beliefs

So far we've explored how our life experiences shape how we react to certain situations in life. In this chapter, we're going to look at just why and how our life experiences imprint upon us in this way. To do so, we are going to draw on some of the valuable work and research of Karl Dawson, the creator of an advanced EFT technique known as Matrix Reimprinting. This is the foundation technique for the Matrix Birth Reimprinting protocol.

Fundamentally, it isn't the experiences themselves that create the greatest proportion of the problem for us. Instead, it is the beliefs that are formed in those moments when we experience something stressful and traumatic. In this chapter, we will explore what beliefs are, how they are formed, and how you can reimprint them so they no longer rule you. First, let's explore the differences between the conscious, subconscious and unconscious minds.

**The conscious mind** is your awareness at this present moment. You are aware of holding this book or sitting on the chair, you are aware of your emotions as you read this book. You may be thinking about what you are going to prepare for dinner and what time you need to pick up the kids from school. Dr Bruce Lipton states that our conscious mind influences our perceptions of the world only 5% of the time. The other 95% is run by our subconscious and unconscious mind.

**The subconscious mind**, or **the preconscious mind**, holds accessible information. You can become aware of this information once you direct your attention to it. Think of this as memory recall. You walk down the street to your house without consciously needing to be alert to your surroundings. You can talk on your mobile and still arrive home safely. You can easily bring to consciousness the subconscious information about the path to your home. You can also easily remember phone numbers that you frequently use.

It is possible that some of what might be perceived to be unconscious becomes subconscious, and then conscious, e.g. a long-forgotten childhood memory suddenly emerges after decades or we ask the subconscious mind to go and find it in the unconscious mind during a session, and then it becomes conscious. We can assume that some unconscious memories need a strong, specific trigger to bring them to consciousness; whereas a subconscious memory can be brought to consciousness more easily.

**The unconscious mind** holds the primitive, instinctual wishes as well as the information that we cannot access (unless we change our state and access these memories using techniques such as Matrix Reimprinting). During our childhood, we acquired countless memories and experiences that formed who we are today. However, we cannot recall most of those memories. They are unconscious forces (beliefs, patterns, subjective maps of reality) that drive our behaviours.[8]

When you have a profound learning experience, this experience is stored away in your subconscious and unconscious minds and *accessed via the matrix*. Some learning experiences are more easily accessible than others, but all these learnings and past events, memories, beliefs, etc, can be moved from the unconscious to the subconscious and into conscious awareness and transformed, changing and creating new neural connections and pathways through our experiences. For the purposes of this book, we will refer to the unconscious mind and subconscious mind as one and call it the subconscious mind, as this is the more generally accepted term.

## How Beliefs are Formed

Beliefs are something that we learn, and quickly they become truths for us. When we have experiences, we reach judgements and therefore conclusions about them, and form beliefs. We end up subconsciously setting them in stone, living by and defending them vehemently, whether they are serving us or not.

Remember what we said in Chapter 2: that there is the actual event that happens and then the story we project onto it. Ten people can witness the same event but each will have their own individual story about what happened because they are filtering it through their thoughts and beliefs.

It might appear that our negative beliefs are working against us, sabotaging our success and destroying our happiness. In reality though, our beliefs are protective mechanisms designed to keep us safe.

Any time you have a threat to survival, a belief is formed in order to protect you from a similar event occurring in the future. A threat to survival sounds like it might be quite a dramatic occurrence, like a car crash, a natural disaster, or somebody pulling a gun on you in the street. Although it includes all of the above (known as Big-T traumas), a threat to survival gets activated on countless occasions from the moment we are conceived.

When we are children, we are truly dependent on our parents for survival and we are hardwired to believe that we will die without them. Any time we feel that they, or other significant adults, cut us off, we can be triggered into a subconscious survival response, particularly if there was not adequate bonding at birth to imprint the sense of safety and belonging (we will talk more about this in Chapter 8).

Have you ever experienced that moment when something occurred and suddenly you felt like you were cut off from yourself? It's as if you'd been totally uprooted. With it comes a really strong sense of separation and 'aloneness' in the world. This is when the survival mechanism has been triggered. If it is triggered significantly or frequently in the womb and the first six years, it can have a high impact on our sense of security and safety, which carries on into adulthood.

In the moment that the survival mechanism is triggered, the subconscious mind draws a conclusion about the world, based on the trigger. 'The world is a dangerous place,' 'I'm unlovable,' 'It's not safe to be me' – whatever conclusion is drawn in that moment, it becomes a blueprint by which we live our life. Just to reiterate an earlier point, the imprinting of our beliefs can come from a major event, or a series of minor events, and we draw conclusions from both of these kinds, that we then live our lives by.

Once these beliefs are formed, we go through life trying to prove that we are right about them. We start to subconsciously look for and gather evidence, selecting situations that confirm what we have learnt about ourselves. We accordingly attract people into our lives who resonate with, and who fit, our perceptions.

Richard Flook, in his book *Why Am I Sick?*[9], highlights the links between physical disease and emotional trauma. He explains that there is a specific type of trauma that has the greatest impact on us, and it is known as a UDIN moment. UDIN is an acronym, coined by Richard Flook, which means

- **U**nexpected
- **D**ramatic
- **I**solating
- and for which we have **N**o strategy to deal with what is happening

UDINs can have dramatic impacts that reverberate throughout our lives.

We have mentioned Big-T traumas, so let's have a look at small-t traumas. These are the events in our lives that are much more common and, although upsetting, they are not classed as life-threatening; however, they can still contain the element that triggers the feeling of being isolated and alone. An example of a small-t trauma is being teased at school or always being picked last for the school team, which can create the belief that 'I'm not good enough'. As a baby at birth, you may hear the doctor or your mother describing you as being an ugly baby because the birthing process has squashed your face. Consequently, you may form the belief you are ugly and unlovable. It is interesting that two people can go through the exact same birth experience or trauma in life, and whilst one may develop a lifelong limiting belief, the other is completely unaffected by it or may develop an empowering belief.

### How are Negative Beliefs Formed?
Our negative beliefs are not just created at a time of trauma – they are also influenced by our family's belief system, by religion and also the culture we are born into. Our parents' beliefs were created by their experiences of life, their environment and also downloaded from their own parents, grandparents, great-grandparents and so forth, going back through the generations.

### Interesting Thought
Before we are conceived, we exist in part as an egg in our mother's ovary. All the eggs a woman will ever carry are formed in her ovaries while she is a foetus of four months. In other words, they are formed in the womb of her mother. This means our cellular life as an egg begins in the womb of our grandmother. Each of us, in part, spent five months in our maternal grandmother's womb and she, in turn, was formed within the womb of her grandmother. As a tiny, pulsating egg, we experience the birth of our mother, the growth of her body, her joys, her fears and her triumphs.

This means there is often a strong connection with our maternal grandmother, as well as our mother, in terms of the way our beliefs are formed.

### Our Early Years
According to Dr Bruce Lipton, cell biologist and bestselling author of *The Biology of Belief*, up to the age of six, children are in what is termed a hypnogogic state, which enables them to download massive amounts of information into the subconscious mind. In order to process self-conscious information, a working database of learned perceptions is

required. Consequently, before a person can express self-consciousness, the brain must go about its primary task of acquiring a working awareness of the world by directly downloading experiences and observations into the subconscious mind. This self-awareness starts to form from the age of seven when the child is able to access a wider range of brain states such as alpha. From birth up to the age of two, the predominate brain wave activity is in the theta range.

From two until six years of age the child's brain state is in delta and theta. These are known as the hypnogogic trance states, and they are the same states as those that hypnotherapists use to directly download new behaviours into the subconscious mind of their clients. A child's perceptions of the world are directly downloaded into the subconscious during this time, without discrimination and without the filters of the analytical self-conscious mind, which doesn't fully exist until age seven. Consequently, our fundamental perceptions about life and our role in it are learnt during a time when we do not have the capacity to choose or reject those perceptions or beliefs. We are simply programmed by what we see and hear. We download our perceptions and beliefs about life years before we acquire the ability for critical thinking. When, as young children, we download limiting or sabotaging beliefs, those perceptions or misperceptions become our truths. If our platform is one of misperception, our subconscious mind will dutifully generate behaviours that are coherent with those programmed truths. Lipton states that the Jesuits were aware of this programmable state and proudly boasted, "Give me the child until it is seven years old and I will give you the man." They knew the child's trance state facilitated a direct implanting of Church dogma into the subconscious mind. Once programmed, that information would inevitably influence 95% of that individual's behaviour for the rest of his or her life.[10]

Let's explore one of the strongest programmes we may have downloaded from our parents, which is that concerning money. I'm using money here, as most of us have very strong beliefs around money and abundance.

1 Take a few moments to think about the beliefs you have about money. Maybe you feel there is never enough, or you feel you do not deserve money or you have beliefs, such as money doesn't grown on trees, you have to work hard for your money, money is dirty, money doesn't make you happy, or it may even burn a hole in your pocket.

2 Now tune into those belief thoughts and ask yourself, "Who do they belong to?" or "Whose voice is that in my head?"

My nan, who experienced rationing during World Wars I and II, taught me that there would always be enough for us to get by, but there would never be anything extra. My father also demonstrated that belief in his behaviour about money, and he kept very tight control on the spending in the house. So that became my belief about money. Saving money or having an abundance of money was difficult until I discovered and transformed those beliefs. I discovered that they didn't even belong to me: they were programmed by my family.

## Beliefs and Our Birth Story

Our current Western paradigm does not generally include the notion that beliefs are formed as soon as we are conceived. Yet our birth story affects us, even if we are not conscious of it. When parents who are intent on having a baby first learn that they have conceived a baby, the mother's body is flooded with bliss and joy chemicals. The unborn child feels the love and receives the message that it is welcome to the world; whereas if a parent's initial response is one of shock and fear, the foetus is likely to subconsciously pick this up and its interpretation can be, 'There is something wrong with me.' This can lead to beliefs around not belonging or not being wanted. (Remember, if you have already conceived a child and did not initially want it, you can tap using the tapping script in the previous chapter to release any emotions that this brings up. You will be releasing them for yourself, and for your child too.)

## Beliefs Formed in the Womb

Some of our strongest beliefs may be created as early as conception. The beliefs that were generated from our parents' reactions when they first found out we were coming into the world are likely to ricochet through every similar experience of our lives. Your first experience of going to the nanny or the nursery, your first day at school, new jobs or projects, moving house – in fact any new experience at all – is probably going to be accompanied by either feelings of joy and anticipation, if that is what your parents felt at the thought of your arrival, or fears or dread and rejection, if that is what you experienced in the womb.

Contrary to popular understanding, if babies are conceived without intention and they are not wanted, on some level they know that. I've worked with so many people (probably somewhere in the thousands) whose mothers went into shock when they found out that they were pregnant. The baby actually holds the shock (and this can be cleared with Matrix Birth Reimprinting). Often when I'm doing a session, you will hear me ask: "Who does that emotion belong to? Who does that shock, fear, worry, anger, belong to?" Nine times out of ten, it actually belongs to the mother or father.

As we mentioned in Chapter 2, because the baby has no power to discern itself as separate from its parents, it takes on their shock as if it was its own.

I worked with a client who was conceived under pretty horrific circumstances that bordered on rape. The mother was very shocked at the time of conception, and didn't want a child. In fact, mentally, the mother was only a child herself. She had no idea how she was going to cope with being a mother. The client had a belief that centred around the feeling that she didn't exist. She sensed that she hadn't been called or invited into being. At the time of conception, the soul starts to connect with the physicality of the egg. Her sense of not being called into being was being recorded in her consciousness. Frequently in cases like this, the belief is formed that 'I shouldn't be here,' or 'I shouldn't exist.'

Often when a life starts like this, the person becomes a risk-taker, has suicidal thoughts or becomes an addict as an adult. A part of them is trying to get to the point of death, because they don't believe that they actually deserve to live. They might also live with a high level of anxiety, accompanied by anger, fear or rage.

Even if the mother decides to keep her baby, there may still be some anger, rage and resentment towards her for not wanting them initially. Conflicting beliefs can end up being created, as the baby holds both the subconscious belief that they were not wanted alongside the love that their mother develops for them.

## Rewriting Beliefs

Conventional talk therapies, although useful for gaining more awareness on where our beliefs have come from, do not actually help us to rewrite them. This is because, in the moment that we experience a trauma, a whole array of sensory information is stored in our subconscious, and it cannot be altered by the conscious mind. The tapping technique, which we explored in the previous chapter, is a highly effective way of accessing this sensory information and releasing it.

There are some core differences between the way we release the sensory information with conventional EFT, and the way we release it with Matrix Reimprinting. With conventional EFT, you recall a trauma you have experienced, and bring all the sensory information of that trauma back into your body so you can release it. Matrix Reimprinting works differently in that it does not bring the information back into the body in order to treat it. Instead, it sees that the information about the event is held in the energetic field (around the body). According to Karl Dawson, the creator of Matrix Reimprinting, because of the overwhelming nature of what happens when we experience a trauma, our subconscious encapsulates the information and we hold that energy in our field. When we are triggered by a similar event, all the thoughts (beliefs), feelings and emotions that are encapsulated in that memory come flooding back; the body responds and is triggered into the fight and flight response to protect us. The downside of this is that we often keep getting triggered over and over again, as our subconscious tries to protect us from what it perceives to be a threat from our environment. Karl has called the encapsulated energy – the part of our consciousness that split off when a trauma was experienced in order to protect us from sensory overwhelm –an ECHO (energetic consciousness hologram).

With Matrix Reimprinting, we can literally go to the moment that our beliefs were created, and rewrite them. Unlike EFT, we don't need to re-experience the accompanying emotion in order to rewrite the belief. Instead, we work with the ECHO outside of the body, in the body field. This means that we don't have to re-experience all the stress and trauma ourselves, as we do with EFT, in order to get peace with it. Still using the EFT tapping technique, we simply step into the memory, tapping on ourselves and the ECHO simultaneously. When we have helped the ECHO release the trauma of what they have experienced, we ask them, "What did you learn about life on that day?" and their answer usually reveals the core belief: 'Something must change for me to be OK,' 'I'm not wanted,' 'I don't belong here,' and so on.

Once we have learnt which belief was formed, we then ask the ECHO what would need to happen for that belief to be different. They can choose any resources they need in order to rewrite the memory or help the ECHO feel empowered. These resources can include tapping on other people who are in the memory, helping them to release the emotion they are feeling; bringing in other people whom they know to support them or calling in spiritual or religious figures (if they are that way inclined). Pets and other animals or objects can also be brought in. The ECHO can bring in anything that is going to enable them to feel safe in the memory so they can rewrite the memory in order for it to become supportive rather than destructive, empowering rather than helpless.

When working with Big-T traumas, we can go into the matrix and start working with the ECHO at any point during the event. We do not have to start at the beginning and work through to the end; sometimes it is better to go straight to the end of the event and work with the ECHO there, letting them know that they survived, that they are safe and helping them to release their shocked and frozen state. We can then freely move to different points of the memory releasing the trauma if needed and finding the beliefs. Remember the UDIN moment when the

ECHO was created? Matrix Reimprinting deals very efficiently with each element of a UDIN moment.

- **U**nexpected – we can prepare the ECHO for the event that is about to happen
- **D**ramatic – we can provide a warning that an event is about to happen and that we can have help and support after the event
- **I**solating – the ECHO no longer feels alone as you are there with them or, as above, others have been brought into the situation to help
- **N**o strategy to deal with what is happening – we can help the ECHO develop a strategy

However, it is important to understand that in this process, you are not denying that any Big-T trauma event ever happened – this would just be avoidance. And in the case of avoidance, the emotional energy and the belief in the memory would still be the same and nothing would change in your life. What you are doing is releasing the stuck emotion and creating a more positive completion to the memory by using your ECHO's imagination to bring about peace. For instance: you may have been born with the cord around your neck and your ECHO may feel panicky. It may have beliefs, such as 'I'm trapped', 'I'm helpless' and 'I'm unsafe in the world'. You are going to tap on your ECHO (your baby self) to help it release the feeling of panic, while at the same time reassuring your ECHO that it survived, as you are living proof of that. Ask your ECHO what it needs in order to feel free, empowered and safe, or in other words, to feel the opposite to how they are feeling. Some ECHOs will choose to unwind the cord themselves, hence empowering themselves; others will choose an angel/doctor/midwife to help them. Whatever they choose, a new picture of freedom and safety will be created and that will become the new belief to reimprint.

If you would like to explore which negative beliefs you currently have, here is a modified exercise called "Brainstorm Your Beliefs", taken from *Transform Your Beliefs, Transform Your Life* by Karl Dawson and Kate Marillat.[11]

## Brainstorm Your Beliefs

Brainstorming your beliefs will give you a conscious understanding of what they are and how strongly they are influencing your life.

1   Look at each of the beliefs on the checklist on page 64 and, in turn, ask yourself, 'How true is that for me out of 100?' (This is known as the 'Validity of Cognition' (VoC) scale.) Write down your VoC score next to each belief. 0% would be 'not true for me at all' and 100% would be 'absolutely true for me'. You will feel a body reaction in one of your emotional centres (heart, stomach, solar plexus) to the ones that really resonate with you.

2   Note your reactions to each belief and brainstorm about where it emerges in different areas of your life and note them down. This will give you information of memories you can work on by yourself or with a qualified practitioner to transform those beliefs.

3   Once you have transformed some of these memories, come back and score the belief again and note anything that has changed.

Feel free to write down and explore any of your own negative beliefs that are not already on this list.

In Chapter 13 we will look at how to get to your subconscious memories of being in the womb and birth. Many of these beliefs could have been created there, but for now work with the memories you consciously remember. You can download this list from the membership site (details given at the back of this book).

| The Belief | How True is This for You? 0 -100% (VoC) |
|---|---|
| I'm not good enough | |
| I'm not lovable | |
| The world is a dangerous place | |
| I'm worthless | |
| I'm incapable | |
| I'm misunderstood | |
| I'm abandoned | |
| I'm betrayed | |
| I'm unattractive | |
| I'm unproductive | |
| I'm incompetent | |
| I'm a failure | |
| I'm a victim | |
| I'm a burden | |
| I'm dumb | |
| I'm always being used | |
| I'm alone | |
| I'm bad | |
| I'm guilty | |
| I'm sinful | |
| I'm confused | |
| I'm trapped | |
| I'm powerless | |
| I'm inferior | |
| I'm separated from God | |
| I don't want to be here | |
| It's not safe to be seen | |

## The Five "F's": Fight, Flight, Freeze, Fainting and Fooling Around

You are probably familiar with fight and flight. When you experience a trauma, two of the most common responses are to fight or flee. Another component, the freeze response, is also a key part of Matrix Reimprinting.

If you run away, or stay and respond through fighting, an ECHO is not usually created. If you can't run away and you can't fight your way out of a situation, then you go into freeze mode. The key thing to understand is that animals in the wild go into freeze repeatedly, but they always shake to release the freeze response. Humans and domesticated animals don't do this, and this is how they end up storing trauma in the form of ECHOs.

I also like to add two other components to the fight, flight and freeze responses. One of them is fainting. If freezing doesn't work and you're still feeling immense danger, then another option is to faint. As a horse lover and owner, I've seen this reaction in horses a few times. When people are trying to load horses into boxes, the first thing the horse will do is put up a fight. Then they will try to run away. Once they start feeling trapped and they can't fight any more and they can't run away, then they go into freeze, with their feet planted firmly at the bottom of the ramp. I actually saw somebody trying to whip a horse to make it go into the box and after it had tried all of the above strategies, it shut down and fainted – it couldn't process what was happening to it and that was the only remaining response it had. I've seen something similar in humans too. I once had a client who would faint if she was triggered into the subconscious memory of her conception and birth trauma. Her story can be read in Chapter 15.

The fifth 'F' is fooling around. Again, like fainting, it is not part of the conventional Matrix Reimprinting teaching, but rather something I have noticed with my work with people.

Did you ever find yourself or someone else making an inappropriate joke in a traumatic moment? Although it might seem like a lack of compassion, the humour is actually a way of disassociating from the traumatic event.

## Matrix Reimprinting and the Freeze Response

The conventional Matrix Reimprinting protocol is designed to rewrite our freeze responses. Any time in life you experienced a freeze, it is most likely that an ECHO was formed; you can use the Matrix Reimprinting protocol to let your system know that the trauma has passed, that it is safe, and all is well.

When we experience the freeze response and an ECHO is created, not only are the emotions and beliefs that we felt at the time locked into that capsule, but also anything that is physically being experienced within our body at that time, such as anaesthetics, drugs, food substances, and any other toxins. The body holds onto them in that moment of freeze. As a massage therapist, I would often find that people not only have a physical release of toxins but also a release of emotion after a massage. Sometimes I can smell anaesthetics on the client's breath when using Matrix Birth Reimprinting with them – similar to massage, that long-held physical substance has finally been released.

Interestingly, if we are eating something at the time that a trauma occurs, we can also become sensitive to that food. In *Matrix Reimprinting Using EFT*, by Karl Dawson and Sasha Allenby, there is a case study of a woman who would go into anaphylactic shock when she smelt coffee. When her practitioner did a Matrix Reimprinting session with her, they discovered that her subconscious mind associated the coffee with danger. She had fled from an abusive partner who had beaten her to within inches of her life. Afterwards she was placed in a women's refuge, where the women sat around, talking about their traumatic experiences and drinking coffee. Her subconscious began to associate the coffee with the trauma. (Incidentally, after the session she was no longer affected by coffee.)

## Carrying Out the Protocol on Yourself

The following is a summary of the classic Matrix Reimprinting technique, adapted from *Transform Your Beliefs, Transform Your Life* by Karl Dawson and Kate Marillat.

1  Find the ECHO
2  Create a safe strategy
3  Tap to release the freeze and other emotions
4  Find the limiting belief
5  Create a new belief
6  Carry out the reimprinting process
7  Measure your success

### Step 1: Find the ECHO

With your eyes closed, focus on a conscious memory you want to work with. Please do not pick anything too traumatic to work with on your own. It is also worth mentioning that what starts out as a small-t trauma can sometimes very quickly link into a Big-T event that holds a lot of emotion, and you could find it difficult to stay dissociated. If you find this happening to you, please find a qualified Matrix Reimprinting practitioner to work with.

### Step 2: Create a Safe Strategy

Assess the memory you have chosen to work with. Does it feel safe to imagine your adult self stepping into the picture? If not, then you have the ability to make it safe by freezing others around your ECHO associated with this memory or moving your ECHO to another place.

Stay dissociated from the ECHO, as this will keep you safe and won't trigger all the negative emotion or energy that they're feeling. This means that you look at your ECHO from the outside and don't 'become' them.

### Step 3: Tap to Release the Freeze and Other Emotions

Step into the picture and ask the ECHO how they are feeling.

Release the freeze response by imagining tapping on the ECHO for their fear or emotion that they are facing.

For example: 'Even though you are panicking, you deeply love and accept yourself.'

You can also add phrases to let your ECHO know that they are safe and create a sense of community.

'It's over.'

'You're safe.'

'I'm here to help.'

'You're not alone.'

### Step 4: Find the Limiting Belief

Ask your ECHO, "What negative belief did you make about yourself and your life on that day?" A sample response could be: "I have to be perfect to be loved."

### Step 5: Create a New Belief

What resources does the ECHO need to create resolution? Often once the emotion is released, your ECHO will start to view what happened differently and the new understanding of what happened creates a natural, new, positive feeling or belief. For instance, if Dad was angry and shouting at you because he was fearful that you were going to hurt yourself, and it wasn't because he didn't love you, now that you have helped your ECHO release the freeze, they have gained that new understanding. You can also explain this to them. When creating the new belief, your ECHO may choose to bring another family member in, or a favourite toy or pet. Let your ECHO have the experience that imprints the new belief.

### Step 6: Carry out the Reimprinting Process

When you have a new picture that represents the belief, take it in through the top of your head and then around all the parts of your body and into your heart. Use your heart to amplify the picture and send it out into the matrix.

### Step 7: Measure your Success

After the reimprinting process, it's time to check in with the original memory.

Close your eyes and tune back into the original memory. What has changed? What work is left to do?

You can go into every memory at least twice, and often many more times, to find the deeper lessons hidden within it.

### Exercise

Practice using the Matrix Reimprinting technique on yourself on a specific memory following the guidelines above – make sure it is not traumatic.

I recommend that you work with a qualified Matrix Reimprinting practitioner for Big-T events. (If you would like to become a practitioner, there are EFT and Matrix Reimprinting trainings in most countries around the world. Go to the resources section at the back of this book to find the practitioner training website for EFT, Matrix Reimprinting and Matrix Birth Reimprinting.)

Now that you have learnt the basics of EFT and Matrix Reimprinting, we will look at your birth stories and how they affect you. Later on in the book we will also learn how to use the Matrix Birth Reimprinting process to transform your birth stories.

Part 2

# The Science Behind
# Matrix Birth Reimprinting

# Chapter 5

# Our Birth Stories

*Mothers intuitively know what scientists have only recently discovered: that the unborn child is a deeply sensitive individual who forms a powerful relationship with his or her parents – and the outside world – while still in the womb.* **Thomas Verny, MD** *Nurturing the Unborn Child* **(1991)**

How we come into the world matters.

In earlier chapters, we highlighted how our beliefs and emotions begin to form as soon as we are conceived. Another element, one of the most significant, is how we actually enter the world. Our birth stories – in other words, the experiences we have when we are born – have a highly significant impact on the way we experience the world. However, it isn't just on the emotional level that we are impacted. The process of our birth not only forms vital beliefs about the way we filter our experiences of the world, but a number of underlying physical processes also start to activate as we are born. Our birth sets us up physically, mentally and emotionally for the life that we are about to lead.

Dr William Emerson, a psychotherapist, workshop leader, writer, lecturer, and pioneer in the field of pre- and perinatal psychology, claims that if you go into his consulting room at the age of, say, 45, he can tell from your physical problems exactly how your birth was. Whether you've got digestive, endocrine or respiratory problems, he'll be able to correlate them with what happened as you were born. Dr Emerson is acutely aware of how our modern birthing processes impact on our health throughout our lives, and in this chapter we'll explore the impact of some of those mechanical birthing processes, as well as how we can undo some of the issues that may have arisen.

It seems to me that understaffing, pressure to perform on a certain time scale, turning birth into a business, and fear of being sued in many hospitals has changed the way many birthing professionals view birth.

In the film *The Business of Being Born*[12], they interviewed many birthing professionals in America and found that they have rarely, or never, seen a natural, unmedicated birth. They are no longer being taught how to birth a breech baby naturally. On a positive note, it has been shown that women who hire a doula (doula: an experienced woman who offers emotional and practical support to a woman (or couple) before, during and after childbirth) and receive continuous support are more likely to have spontaneous vaginal births and less likely to have any pain medication, epidurals, negative feelings about childbirth and less likely to have other medical interventions such as forceps and C-sections. Women who have a doula attending the birth can reduce the risk of C-section by 28%; it has been shown that the labours are shorter by about 40 minutes and their babies are less likely to have a low Apgar score at birth.[13]

A client who had recently had a traumatic birth told me she felt that things had started to go wrong for her right at the start of labour before she had even got to the hospital. She told me of her anger because the doula she had booked to attend her birth said that she was too busy to come to the house, and to call her back when she got to the hospital and the labour was well underway. This was not what my client had expected, as most doulas will be there with you right from the beginning of the labour.

The presence of birth attendants can have a dramatic effect on whether a birth is natural and safe or traumatic. There are many wonderful birth attendants who are compassionate and understanding and know what it takes to create the right supportive environment for a successful birth.

Unfortunately, many of our midwives here in the UK are becoming highly stressed. They are coming under increasing pressure to perform, there is a lack of staffing and lack of funding from the NHS and they are struggling to take the time necessary to be present with mothers as they would normally be. Also, some birthing attendants may have their own trauma around birth and are not able to be fully present with the mother. The mother may sense there is something wrong with her or the baby by how they are responding or not responding to her and may feel out of control and fearful for her own and the baby's safety. I have heard many reports of mothers being spoken to harshly and even of some being verbally abused; they are made to feel like they are doing something wrong and that they are worthless. In many of these cases, the mother can go into the fear response; pain will increase due to the release of stress hormones such as adrenaline. Adrenaline contracts the circular muscles of the uterus – including the cervical opening, which must relax to dilate. This contraction results in pain and impaired circulation, often causing foetal distress.[14] This can stop or slow labour and medical intervention will be needed.

There is still much progress to be made in the Western world to assist women to be able to have a natural and unhindered birth. We need to start by reminding mothers that a natural birth is possible, by teaching the medical staff how to carry out a natural birth and by providing staff with the appropriate time and facilities, so they can fully support the mother. This is key to ensuring that our future babies come into the world un-traumatised by their birth experience, on both an emotional and physical level.

## The Physical Impact of the Birthing Process
The birth process is, in itself, highly sophisticated in design. In our Western medical model, we have become desensitized to the level of intricacy involved in this process. The Western medical model tends to view the birth process as a mechanical one whose sole purpose is to get the baby out into the world. But the process itself is much less mechanical than we have been entrained to believe. It is designed to activate a number of systems, including our immune, endocrine, digestive and respiratory systems, and thus has a major impact on our health and wellbeing.

There are a number of elements of this process that are overlooked or misunderstood, and the primary one includes what happens when we come down the birth canal and the role of the umbilical cord.

## The Birth Canal

In a 'natural birth', as we come down the birth canal, our bodies are massaged with contractions. Besides serving the physical purpose of helping us enter into the world, these contractions also activate the immune system.

As the baby comes down the birth canal, it picks up all the natural digestive enzymes that it needs from its mother. These are swallowed and go into the digestive tract. Babies born by C-section don't get these enzymes, and they don't have the added bonus of having their body massaged. The massage also stimulates the lungs. That's why most C-section babies have trouble breathing to begin with, because they haven't had that gentle massaging experience.

In some cases, a C-section is vital for preserving the lives of the mother and baby. However, in more recent years, it has become fashionable to opt for a C-section in place of a natural birth, as part of the birthing plan. This is one of the many ways that we have become disconnected from some of the essential elements of the natural birthing process, and it has implications for the immunity of babies who experience a C-section.

## The Umbilical Cord

The umbilical cord also plays more of a vital role than we have come to credit it for. Most of us think that the role of the umbilical cord is just to supply oxygen and nutrients to the foetus in the womb. However, when we are born, our lungs are flat because they have no air in them. The first breath that the baby takes begins to inflate the lungs with air, and all the blood capillaries that support the lungs start filling with blood. During this time, the baby is still being supplied with vital oxygen through the umbilical cord.

In fact, the umbilical cord ideally needs to remain connected for around 20 minutes after birth, until the lungs have become fully activated.

During this time, the cord pulsates, and the baby receives an extra 30% of its blood supply. The blood coming in through the cord provides further oxygen. So if the baby is having trouble breathing because it has mucus down its throat, for example, then the cord ensures that it is still receiving oxygen.

The baby also receives stem cells from the cord – these are needed to set up its immune system. This means that when you leave the cord connected, the baby's immunity gets stronger. It is no coincidence that the cord, intact, is long enough so that the baby can be lifted to the mother's chest. And if the baby, on its mother's chest, can immediately start to suckle, the colostrum from the breast milk, which aids in fighting infection, establishes further immunity.

While the baby is in the womb, they don't need this extra 30% of blood supply, but when they enter world, they do, in order to give them the best chance of survival.

The challenge is that the current Western mechanical birthing paradigm has become alienated from the importance of nature's design. The cord is often cut within 10 seconds of birth, meaning that the baby loses out on valuable nutrients and oxygen.

The risks associated with early cord clamping are:
- Hypotension (low blood pressure)
- Hypovolaemia (low blood volume)
- Anaemia (low haemoglobin/iron)
- Hypoglycaemia (low blood sugar)
- Metabolic acidosis
- Respiratory Distress Syndrome
- Hypothermia (low body temperature when deprived of warm blood flow through the cord)
- Higher incidence of cardiac murmurs in the first 14 days of life
- Suboptimal flow of blood to the gastrointestinal tract, increasing risk of necrotising enteritis in preterm babies
- Brain damage, including possibly cerebral palsy and autism, if the baby is asphyxiated

The benefits of delayed cord clamping include:
- 50% larger red cell volume, enlarged blood volume, protection from anaemia
- Increased amounts of white blood cells and antibodies, which help the baby to fight off infections
- Increased platelets, which are important in normal blood clotting
- Increased plasma proteins and other nutrient benefits that come with adequate perfusion
- Better blood circulation in the first few hours after birth
- A normal temperature can be more easily maintained
- The baby receives his or her own stem cells. These may contribute to health and wellbeing in ways we do not fully understand yet[15]

## Birth Trauma

When we understand that the baby is indeed a conscious and feeling being, the tradition of holding them upside down and smacking them seems barbaric. Put your adult mind into that experience for a moment. You've just transitioned into a brand-new world and all of a sudden you're being held upside down and smacked. You hear loud noises, sometimes shouting, bright lights, your body is being moved, roughly handled and held in ways you have not experienced before. You experience pain from an injection, a tube is forced down your throat suctioning out fluid. You are washed in water that is not your body temperature or the temperature of the womb where you have just come from. In fact, a baby's body temperature is actually 1 degree higher than our normal body temperature and you can put the baby into shock by putting it in water that is too warm or too cold.

According to a 1995 study by Dr William Emerson, 95% of all the births in the United States can be classified as traumatic. 50% were rated as moderate trauma and 45% as severe. Currently around 4 million babies[16] are born every year in the US: that ultimately means a high volume of traumatised babies entering the world.

Now that we have looked at the intricacies of the birthing process and how we negatively impact this process with our Western medical procedures, in the following chapter we will discuss the development of the brain and how these procedures negatively impact it.

# Chapter 6

# The Development of the Brain

*The greatest terror a child can have is that he is not loved, and rejection is the hell he fears. I think everyone in the world to a large or small extent has felt rejection. And with rejection comes anger, and with anger some kind of crime in revenge for the rejection, and with the crime guilt – and there is the story of mankind.* **John Steinbeck**

The formation of the brain in the womb and childbirth shapes and influences the way the baby perceives the world.

It is an obvious fact that your baby's brain forms while it is in the womb. In this chapter we are going to explore the various aspects of brain formation, and how an emotional trauma experienced in the womb can affect the way your baby filters and perceives life.

It is not possible to examine childbirth without exploring how it shapes our beliefs about ourselves and the world. If we have a birth that instils within us a sense of safety, then we will be implanted with the belief that the world is a safe place. In contrast, if we have a traumatic birth, and our separation from our mother is not handled sensitively, then the opposite is true, and we can end up programmed with the belief that the world is a dangerous place. How we relate to the world and how we act in the world from that point on is determined by our birth experience.

The Western medical paradigm creates many challenges for both mothers and babies. If the mother is given the synthetic form of the hormone oxytocin (which goes by the brand name of Pitocin or

Syntocinon) to stimulate the contractions, this can create a shock for the baby and stops the natural production of oxytocin from the mother's body. If left to nature, it is the baby itself who actually initiates the start and the pace of the birthing process, by secreting protein from its lungs into the mother's body.[17]

Now imagine the opposite scenario. The baby is resting in the womb and all of a sudden the birthing process is initiated violently with powerful contractions created by a drug. The contractions aren't allowed to build up in gentle waves. Think tidal wave as opposed to gentle waves lapping up against the shore! With no lead-up to the start of labour, the experience can be shocking, and the baby can be instilled with a sense of powerlessness, which also impacts on later life.

In my work, I have often found that babies who were sped up with Pitocin get frustrated when they are rushed as children. Imagine the scenario. There you are, the parent, running late. You've got to get your older child to school and your 2 year-old is dawdling around the house. As soon as you try and hurry her up, she throws a tantrum. The reason that she does can be because what you are actually doing is pressing on that trigger of being rushed when she had to leave her first home.

As an aside, if a baby is overdue, there is often an underlying fear of being born that is holding them back. This can include the baby's own fear of coming into the world or the mother's fear of giving birth or of being a parent. Many clients that I have worked with who were overdue say that they didn't want to be born. We can address this with the Matrix Birth Reimprinting protocol and we will explore this in Chapter 12.

### Environmental Conditioning

Much of the conditioning we experience is environmental; in other words, we download the world around us as though it was the truth. If the baby is born into a highly traumatic environment, this can have a significant impact.

One of my clients was born during World War II in a London air-raid shelter. She had extended her energy field out into the environment around her, so not only was she picking up on her mother, but also on everyone from miles around her. In life, she became hypervigilant and was very influenced by her surroundings. Nowhere felt safe to her until we created a safe place for her to be born with the Matrix Birth Reimprinting protocol.

From my experience, I know that we are all empathic to our surroundings whether we are conscious of it or not. We not only tune into the energetic fields of our family, but also those of our ancestors, our culture, the human collective consciousness, and also the energies of the earth.

## Three Trimesters And Brain Development
It's not only our birthing experience that shapes the brain, though. During pregnancy, the brain develops in the womb, and each developmental stage can impact the beliefs of the child, depending on what is going on in its surroundings as it develops.

### First Trimester – the Reptilian Brain
During the first trimester, the reptilian brain forms. This is the action and protection brain. It is the part that gets triggered into fight, flight or freeze. It activates our protection mechanisms for survival.

The reptilian brain is concerned about what is happening right now, in the present. Because it is primarily wired for survival, it isn't focused on what went before or what is yet to come. It is the part of us that gets triggered on matters of life or death. If we are being chased by a tiger (or a mugger, which is more likely in the Western world), it is this part of the brain that activates to get us out of danger.

This part of the brain is the oldest and most primal part of our brain systems. It controls the body's vital functions such as heart rate, breathing, body temperature and balance. It is linked to our sexual tendencies, our sense of territorialism, nesting and food.

In order to understand this part of the brain better, think of a male lizard. He sees something moving in the distance. He is going to want to know whether he is in danger or not. Is the thing that is moving towards him a threat? Perhaps something that is going to eat or kill him? If it is

82

another male lizard then he will be going to want to know whether he needs to defend his territory. If it's a female, he is going to want to know whether he'll be able to mate with her. Or perhaps the thing that is moving towards him is something that he can eat to survive. Outside of these concerns, nesting and whether he has got somewhere safe to sleep at night would be his only other needs.

The reptilian brain functions in a similar way in humans. When we are triggered into survival – when something in our external reality registers as a threat to our safety – the reptilian brain activates in order to protect us. You may have had more than one experience where it feels like you lost your centre or forgot yourself in the face of a particular threat and you wanted to get away from the situation. Perhaps you seemed to suddenly behave like an automated version of yourself. If you did, that was your reptilian brain taking over.

When the reptilian brain is triggered, the response is entirely subconscious. You don't have to think about it for it to activate. In fact, it activates independently of your conscious mind.

During the first trimester, the reptilian brain develops and much of the baby's creative energy is focused on this formation at that time. If the baby experiences a life or death situation then, it can create a strong imprint on the reptilian brain, causing the survival mechanisms to be very sensitive to triggering even when we are safe, later in life.

And it isn't just a threat to the baby's survival that will trigger this sensitivity in the first trimester. If the mother is frequently triggered into survival during this time, either because her own reptilian brain is similarly sensitive, or she is in a highly anxious state about the baby's wellbeing, or she experiences either small-t or Big-T trauma, the development of the baby's reptilian brain will also be impacted.

If you are reading this after your first trimester of pregnancy (whether or not your baby is already born), and you find yourself fretting about what might have unfolded at that time, the Matrix Birth Reimprinting protocol that we are going to learn in Chapter 12 can rewrite the heightened sense of trauma that may have been imprinted then. Whether your baby is still in the womb or already born, you can do the technique on their behalf to release the trauma response and create a sense of safety and wellbeing. On countless occasions, I have seen this heal the belief that there is a threat to safety and survival.

## Second Trimester – the Limbic Brain

During the second trimester of pregnancy, the limbic or mammalian brain develops. The limbic brain sits on top of the reptilian brain. Whereas the reptilian brain is your action and protection brain, the limbic brain is often referred to as your emotional brain. Not only is it the part of the brain that is associated with emotions, but it also houses our inherent intelligence for nurturing. It is the part of the brain that gets activated during bonding (which we will discuss in Chapter 8).

The limbic system is made up of a number of parts, some of which we will discuss here.

**Thalamus** – the portion of the brain that is responsible for detecting and relaying information from our senses (smell, hearing and sight); it's directly linked to the cerebrum, which is the section of the brain that is responsible for thinking and movement.

**Hypothalamus** – the part of the brain that is responsible for producing multiple chemical messengers, called hormones. These hormones control water levels in the body, sleep cycles, body temperature, and food intake.

**Cingulate Gyrus** – serves as a pathway that transmits messages between the inner and outer portion of the limbic system and is activated during the bonding process.

**Amygdala** – responsible for preparing the body for emergency situations. It assists in the development of memories, especially emotional and crisis, and also plays a major role in pleasure and sexual arousal.

**Hippocampus** – responsible for converting short-term memories into long-term memories and works closely with the amygdala.

As we have discussed, the limbic brain is related to smell and hearing. After we are born, a smell will often trigger a memory, and the part of the brain that is getting triggered is the thalamus in the limbic brain. For example, you may smell lavender and think of your grandmother, because she always wore lavender perfume. Smells are often linked to emotions because of the way they are stored in the limbic brain. The smell will bypass the conscious brain and go directly to the emotional brain. There is a similar response to hearing things. If you had previously escaped a fire and you hear fire alarms, for example, fear will instantly be triggered, adrenaline will be released and you will usually go into fight or flight. Remember the thalamus is linked to the cerebrum, which controls movement.

Just like the reptilian brain, the mammalian brain is focused on the present. But unlike the reptilian brain, it also relates to the past. Something from your external reality can trigger the limbic brain, whether it is something that you see, hear, smell, touch or taste. When something of this nature reminds you of an earlier traumatic life experience, it is the limbic brain that responds. It is trying to protect you from the same event occurring again. But in the case of trauma, it can become overly sensitive, particularly if the impact of the traumatic memory is not released from the limbic brain. (Tools such as EFT, Matrix Reimprinting and Matrix Birth Reimprinting aid in the release of the impact.)

In order to understand the mammalian brain, it can help to think of a mammal such as a monkey. Compare the way a monkey behaves to the behaviour of a lizard. As we discussed earlier, a lizard's main concerns are safety, mating, eating, territory and nesting. You will not witness a lizard having an emotional response to any of these concerns, but rather, you will find him managing his survival responses. The monkey is different. If you have observed a group of monkeys for any period of time, you will notice they react emotionally. You know when a monkey is angry, sad, fearful or frustrated. These responses come from the mammalian brain. That's why, if you were to visit the zoo, you would likely feel a closer empathy with monkeys than you would with lizards, because you can relate to the feelings they are experiencing.

Because of the way the limbic brain is also related to the past, you will find that monkeys have been 'programmed' by their past experiences. They will have emotional responses about the life that has gone before.

Not only is the limbic brain connected with our memories and our learning – it also controls all our relationships within our body environment. It's the part of the brain that controls our immunity and self-healing system. It also controls our hormonal system, which is why our hormones are so closely linked with emotions such as love, hate, rage.

The limbic brain is also the part of the brain that gets associated with addictions. If you learn to reward yourself when you are in an emotional state, you can become emotionally dependent on food, alcohol or drugs: the limbic brain is linking the emotion with the reward of the substance in question. Pacify the emotion with food or drugs enough times, and as soon as you feel the emotion, it will trigger the desire for the same food or drug. That trigger is being activated in the limbic brain.

Think back to the baby in the womb. During the second trimester, the mother's emotional state is going to be influencing the development of the limbic brain. The pregnancy itself is already going to be affecting the emotional state of the mother, because of the link between hormones and the limbic brain. But if there are circumstances outside of the pregnancy that are creating a heightened and prolonged emotional response in the mother during the second trimester of pregnancy, this is going to affect how the baby's limbic brain develops, and their response to emotions later in life. (Once again, these cases can be reimprinted with Matrix Birth Reimprinting and we will learn how to do this in Chapter 12.)

### Third Trimester – the Neocortex, also known as the new Mammalian or Verbal-intellectual Brain

In the third trimester, the neocortex forms. This part of the brain sits on top of the emotional brain or the limbic system. It is what we term our conscious mind. It is our higher intelligent mind and it connects to our language and our conscious thinking. The other main functions of the neocortex are: sensory perception, generation of motor commands, and spatial reasoning (mental manipulation of 2-dimensional and 3-dimensional figures – our brain's ability to mentally visualise moving objects in order to help understand what they are and where they belong).[18]

Foetuses are developing their intellectual skills. In our current Western medical paradigm, we assume that babies don't start learning language until well after they are born. However, in the third trimester the baby starts learning languages from hearing sounds from the mother and father. Sound carries easily through the amniotic fluid in the womb and is also carried through the mother's bone structure.

Although babies obviously cannot speak when they are in the womb, they are picking up on the phonetics of languages, so they hear how words or letters are pronounced. This is part of their socio-cultural programming, and whatever language they have heard in the womb, they are able to learn it more easily than one they haven't. If the mother is profoundly deaf and mute, then quite often the baby will have difficulty learning languages as the structures in the brain that are prewired to respond to language will not have been stimulated.[19] It's in this third trimester when this part of the brain gets activated.

How do we know that babies are learning while they're in the womb? An experiment was carried out where a mother was asked to sing a certain nursery rhyme to her baby over and over again for a week. After a week of repeating the same nursery rhyme, they strapped the mother to a foetal heart monitor and asked her to sing a variety of different nursery rhymes. When she sang the one she had been singing for a week, the baby's monitor started to flash. The baby began moving around, indicating that it was able to identify the songs that its mother had been repeating.[20]

A similar experiment was carried out with the theme tune of a popular UK soap opera. When the mother had a good feeling watching her favourite TV programme, the baby also recognised this as a feel-good time. The baby in the womb would respond to the theme tune being played.[21] (If you are pregnant, and you play certain songs when you're going to bed, it is believed that it is a good way for the baby to learn to associate that tune with rest time. So if you have some music that you find really relaxing that helps you go to sleep, you can also play it when the baby is born.)

The neocortex can access the past, the present and the future.

When you are worrying about the future, the part that is triggering the worrying is actually your limbic or emotional brain, but you're also projecting into the future using your neocortex.

To recap, there are three different brain parts developed in utero. Firstly, we have the reptilian brain (our survival and action brain), which is the oldest part of our brain. Just like the dinosaurs and other reptiles, it goes back the furthest. Secondly, we have the limbic, or emotional, brain, present in all mammals, which appeared later in our evolution. Thirdly, we have the neocortex (our thinking brain), which is present in more evolved mammals, such as dolphins, monkeys, horses, dogs and humans.

## The Prefrontal Cortex

The fourth part of our brain structure is the prefrontal cortex. It sits in our forehead behind our eyes. In evolutionary terms, it is the most recent part of our brain.

This part of our brain is stimulated during the birthing process; it begins to develop at birth and not in the womb. It is the part that is dependent on the bonding experience and it is shaped by the child's environment. When the baby is born, the growth and the connection of the prefrontal cortex are further activated.

One of the roles of the prefrontal cortex is to govern the left and right hemispheres of the brain. It connects the logical (left) side of your brain with the creative (right) side. These two parts of the brain, connected, are responsible for what is known as the 'civilised mind'. As adults, it gives us the ability to reason and make choices. It is also linked with self-control, self-compassion and empathy. We will explore this further in this chapter and Chapter 8 when we look at how babies who don't have the bonding experience may not develop the prefrontal cortex and consequently don't develop empathy or compassion.

## More on Brain Formation and the Womb

In each of the sections above we touched upon what might happen in the womb at these various stages of brain development. Just to reiterate, the chronic or continuously held negative or positive emotions of the mother affect the development of the baby's brain. Dr Bruce Lipton highlights this in *The Biology of Belief*. If the mother is living in fear of her life, then the foetus will develop a larger reptilian brain with a stronger sense of survival. The fight or flight instincts will then be easily triggered and this will continue throughout childhood and adulthood.

If the mother and baby are living in a supported environment, then the prefrontal cortex and the neocortex will be able to develop with higher intelligence. More of the developmental energy goes into these parts of the brain creating a more peaceful, compassionate and intelligent human. However, if the environment is fraught with fear and danger, then the prefrontal cortex and neocortex will not develop in the same way. This is why children living in socially and economically deprived households often do not thrive emotionally and mentally. Because the reptilian and mammalian brains are being constantly triggered and the neocortex is not given the support to develop, the higher intelligence centres do not get the chance to evolve.

### Mr X – Case Study

Imagine that you are sitting in a bar. You get chatting with a guy who starts telling you his birth story.

The first thing he tells you is that his father died of cancer while he was four months in utero. His mother suddenly went into grief from losing her husband. Two months later, when he was six months in utero, his 12-year-old brother also died of cancer. His mother went into major depression. She tried unsuccessfully to both abort her baby and then to kill herself.

As soon as the baby was born, the mother couldn't cope, so she gave the baby away to her brother. From birth to three years of age, he lived with his uncle, before returning to live with his mother, who had by then remarried. As soon as he returned to the family home, his stepfather began physically and psychologically abusing him. He lived with this abuse for six years before being handed back to his uncle.[22]

So the guy in the bar is actually pretty well known. You may have heard of him. His name is Saddam Hussein. Of course, this story does not excuse his actions, but it does explain them somewhat. Hussein was a failed abortion baby who experienced continued abuse and emotional neglect as a child.

Dr Jerrold M. Post's book, *Leaders and Their Followers in a Dangerous World*, explores how Hussein was extremely self-absorbed, paranoid, lacking constraints of conscience with a willingness to use whatever means necessary to accomplish his goals. Post highlights that people like Hussein have little empathy for the pain and suffering of either their enemies or their own people.[23]

My guess is that if we carried out a post-mortem, his prefrontal lobes would have been underdeveloped.

It is also interesting to note that Adolf Hitler had similar prenatal experiences to those of Saddam Hussein. John C. Sonne writes in his article, "On Tyrants as Abortion Survivors", how Adolf's father, Alois, beat his mother, Klara, when she was pregnant with him, and continued to beat Klara, Adolf and his siblings throughout his childhood.[24] Sonne also goes on to say that Francisco Franco, Joseph Stalin, Benito Mussolini, Slobodan Milosevic, Osama bin Laden, and Klebold and Harris, the Columbine school killers, could also fit the profile of abortion survivors.

> Abortion survivors are persons who have experienced the threat of being aborted, either from direct physical attempt, or from having lived in an unwelcoming prenatal environment in which abortion was contemplated consciously or unconsciously by one or both parents, and/or significant others, even though not acted out directly.[25]

Sonne also states that:

> Not all persons threatened with abortion become murderous tyrants, or even symptomatic. Whether or not they become symptomatic depends on the severity of the threat, upon their innate resilience, and whether or not in later life they are further traumatised, or have healing,

loving and growth promoting experiences. Many abortion survivors become loving, contributing members of society, and good parents.[26]

In my experience, some of the best healers are the ones who have experienced early childhood trauma.

### Development of the Child's Brain

Although this is a book on Matrix Birth Reimprinting, it can also help to be aware of the continued brain development after the child is born.

James W. Prescott, PhD is a developmental neuropsychologist and cross-cultural psychologist. He initiated a number of brain research programmes with baby monkeys, which documented that the early life experiences of separating mother and infant induced a variety of developmental brain abnormalities. Prescott believes that the failure to bond in the mother-infant relationship, including insufficient breastfeeding, induces developmental brain abnormalities in the infant/child that result in the later depression and violence of suicidal and homicidal behaviours that are of epidemic proportions in America; they can also account in part for the prevalence of the massive psychiatric medication of the children and youth of America.[27]

The baby needs touch and movement stimulation for healthy emotional brain development. We will explore the importance of movement later on in this chapter.

Prescott stated in an article called "Sensory Deprivation in the Developing Brain" by Michael Mendizza that:

> If we have pleasurable sensory stimulation then the memory traces (Engrams) are stored as templates that will be images of pleasure. If they are painful they are going to be stored as images of pain. And pain evokes violent responses. But there is something else that invokes violent responses – the absence of pleasure – and that's different than the sensory event of pain, and most people don't appreciate that distinction. In fact, more damage occurs with the sensory deprivation of pleasure than the actual experience of physical, painful trauma,

which, in fact, can be handled quite well in individuals who have been brought up with a great deal of physical affectional bonding and pleasure, which carries with it emotional trust and security. So we really have to look at the trauma of sensory deprivation of physical pleasure and that translates into the separation experiences, the isolation experiences of the infant from the mother, that's the beginning.[28]

I have found that most of my long-term clients are those who were continually emotionally neglected as babies and young children. We know that the feeling of isolation is the most damaging, as separation means potential death to the child. We will be dealing with separation more in Chapter 9.

As with all traumatic events, the first thing that happens when we carry out Matrix Reimprinting with our younger self is that we are bringing in that much needed connection. Creating safety and connection is essential to our baby self. It can bring about the changes we need, to begin to heal isolation and rebuild our feeling of connection.

The second phase of the development of the brain after birth follows the same order as it develops in the womb. First comes the further development of the reptilian brain, from birth to up to seven years old. From birth to the first year, most of the energy goes into the development of the reptilian brain and promoting the need for food, safety, nurturing, warmth and love.

At the age of one, the limbic or emotional brain begins to develop. By eighteen months of age, the toddler has as many neural fields available as we have as adults.[29] During this time, the toddler starts experiencing a great range of emotions. This development continues into the second year. Quite often this time is referred to as 'the terrible twos'. The hormone system begins to develop and engage simultaneously, which accounts for the mood swings that a toddler usually experiences.

By the time the child is four years old, the right hemisphere of the brain, which is the creative side, begins to become more active. This is the part of the brain that gets activated through play and imagination. It is not until the child is seven years old that the left hemisphere – which is associated with our intellectual capacity – begins to develop. This explains why stimulating the child through play in the early years is essential. In fact, some schools of thought believe that counting, spelling and other intellectual activities do not need to begin until the child is seven years old, because of the later development of the intellectual brain. If the child is encouraged to focus the majority of its attention on play-related learning such as colouring, drawing, puzzles, listening to and engaging in stories, and anything else that requires imagination, the creative brain is allowed to flourish. In situations where the parents push the child with more structured learning during this period, the left or intellectual brain will develop early, but at the expense of the creative brain. This can result in a child who is intellectual or logical, but has little imagination or creative capacity.

In some cases, activities where the right brain and left brain are activated simultaneously are useful. For example, a child who is learning music will engage the left side of their brain for the learning aspect, and the right side for the creative aspect.

Another key component in understanding brain development is that up until the age of six or seven, a child does not see itself as separate from the world. Spiritual teachers for thousands of years have taught us that there is no separation. Interestingly, a child perceives the world in a similar way (although they are not consciously aware that they do). When the left or logical brain comes online, the child starts realising that the world isn't just about them and them alone. If you recall, in Chapter 4, we highlighted how most of our limiting beliefs are formed in the first six years. In those early years, we do not have the ability to reason, and this is something that we develop around six or seven years of age.

Imagine a 3-year-old boy. He's playing on his lounge floor in front of the television and his dad's watching a programme. The little boy gets up, wanting to show his dad something – maybe he's just finished a jigsaw puzzle or drawn a picture – something he is really excited about and wants to share. Unfortunately, he is standing right in his father's line of vision, and his father is reacting angrily to the football scores. Our little boy doesn't have the capacity to understand that the anger is being directed towards what's happening on television. All he sees and feels is his father's anger. He makes a decision that it must have been due to what he's just finished and that he's done something wrong. If the activity that he had been engaged in was a creative one, that could be enough to stifle his creativity for future activities. At this age, all the mental activity and processing tells the child that everything is personal.

## The Prefrontal Cortex and Teenagers

The prefrontal cortex also relates to socialisation. It's about being connected with other people, bonding, and being compassionate. Teenagers who did not bond with their parents when they were born have a higher chance of actually going on to being violent teenagers.[30] They often have a lot of anger, rage and lessened ability to access compassion. They also have less self-awareness and they lack the understanding of how other people are feeling. This is one of the reasons why, outside of the changes in hormonal responses that are linked to the emotional brain, some teenagers can go into violent rages. It seems to me that when something triggers them emotionally, they go straight into action without subconsciously running by their cognitive brain to check if this action is appropriate.

We discover from Joseph Chilton Pearce's work, *The Biology of Transcendence*, the importance of the baby and child's environment to the development of the brain. He writes about the importance of the bonding process at birth, and also shares that there are other optimal bonding times during a child's life – and one of these times is when we are teenagers.

Around about the age of 14 or 15, we may have our first love, and that's our first experience of bonding with a person who is not our mother or father. If you think about it, it is also the time that males can also end up in gangs, and when they do, they bond with each other. The connection within the group makes them feel loved, accepted, wanted and sometimes powerful.

This is the time when teenagers tend to not want to bond so much with their parents – they bond more with their friends. It's a natural part of the development process for teenagers to start building their ability to bond and connect with others. It is preparing them to leave home and become an independent adult. (As an aside, because they don't necessarily understand this process, parents often perceive that something has gone wrong when the teenager doesn't want to be bonded with them in the same way as before. They often look to fix this instead of allowing this process to play out naturally.)

## Movement and the Development of the Brain

Much of the development of the reptilian brain in the first year is dependent on how the baby is both moved around physically, and also how it is nurtured. In an ideal scenario the baby would be carried in a sling, as this is the most effective way to stimulate the reptilian brain. You may have seen how a baby will often sleep peacefully until you put it down in a cot (crib). The baby inherently knows that its survival depends on being close to its mother. This does not just include being held in the mother's arms, but also being moved around with her. If a sling is used, the baby is kept close to the mother's heart field and is also able to see the face of its mother, enabling a further sense of security (something we will explore further in the next chapter). As humans, we can only be in one of the following two states at any one time: survival or thriving. Survival is a stress-based state, triggered by the reptilian brain when we subconsciously believe that there is a threat to our life. When we are triggered into survival, cortisol levels rise in our body, we release stress hormones, and our digestion becomes compromised. The more our survival response is triggered, particularly in the first six years, the more likely we are to form stress patterns in later life. In contrast, the more we are given the message that we are safe and secure by being in close proximity to our mother, the more we can thrive. If our reptilian brain is constantly being triggered into a state of survival, it will develop a sensitivity to being retriggered later in life.

## Consequences of not Moving the Baby

The studies done on baby monkeys by James Prescott, which we mentioned before, led him to conclude that there are links between being depressed and violent as a teenager and not having bonded or been nurtured as a baby. I do not condone animal experiments, but nonetheless, the studies carried out by Prescott with baby monkeys reveal what happens when they were taken from their mothers and reared in isolation. Some were reared on a static plastic bottle covered in fur fabric and the others on a similar fur-covered bottle that was attached to a swinging rope. The monkeys reared with the swinging fur-covered bottle did not develop any of the emotional socio-psychopathologies that the other monkeys exhibited. Those raised on the static bottle were depressed and withdrawn. They showed autistic behaviours and developed a tendency to rock back and forth. They exhibited violent behaviour as they became juveniles and adults. They also did not want to be touched or held by others. In addition, they had an impaired sense of danger when introduced to an alpha male, and would even attack this male.[31]

It has been noted that children in orphanages in Romania will often show the same rocking behaviour that was common in the isolated monkeys. It is apparent that they are trying to self-soothe and stimulate their own brain connections independently, in the absence of the mother.[32]

## Why Movement is Essential

If you think about what happens in utero, aside from when the mother is sleeping or resting, the baby is always in motion. After the baby is born, the sensory systems – seeing, hearing, smelling, touching and tasting – are all continuously stimulated when the baby is moved around with the mother. The sensory systems are considered non-functional (in other words, we can live without them being stimulated). However, if they aren't stimulated, it can lead to sensory deprivation in the baby.

Rhythmic movements help the baby to integrate primitive reflexes. These are repetitive, automatic movements that are essential for the development of muscle tone and head control, as well as sensory integration and development. Our primitive reflexes form the foundation for our postural, lifelong reflexes, and they need to be integrated by the baby so they can be inactive unless they are needed. In other words, when the baby has practiced its movements and is able to control them, the primitive reflexes are no longer needed, and become inactive. If they remain active, because the baby has not had adequate practice of movement, all sorts of challenges can occur in both childhood and adulthood. Rhythmic Movement Training International™ lists a whole host of conditions that can be initiated if the primal reflexes aren't integrated. These can include ADD/ADHD, autism, learning challenges, developmental delay, sensory integration disorders, vision and hearing challenges, behaviour challenges, extreme shyness, lack of confidence, addiction, inefficient and effortful striving, and constant feelings of overwhelm.[33]

Wearing the baby in a sling helps to integrate all of the reflexes. There are two methods for working with your baby's reflex integration. These are the Masgutova Method created by Dr Masgutova and Rhythmic Movement Training (RMT). Details can be found in the Bibliography at the end of the book.

Now that we have explored the development of the brain in pregnancy, birth and childhood, in the next chapter we will explore heart intelligence, and its role in pregnancy and childbirth.

# Chapter 7

# The Importance of the Heart

*It matters not who you love, where you love, why you love, when you love, or how you love. It matters only that you love.* **John Lennon**

We have been entrained to believe that our intelligence comes from our brain. This entrainment includes the belief that when we need to make a decision, we must meticulously think it through. Our cultural entrainment to be head-centred has dulled our connection with one of our most vital resources – the heart.

Human intelligence is actually heart-centred. It is based on our intuition and innate knowing and not on our thought processes. In this chapter we will explore this paradigm shift, along with its effects on our perception of how babies experience the world.

### The Intelligence of the Heart

HeartMath Institute is a research and education organisation that investigates the science of the heart, stress reduction and emotional self-regulation. A whole series of studies have been carried out by the HeartMath Institute on the energy of the heart's field and the link between the brain and the body. Scientists have found that the heart is the most powerful generator of electromagnetic energy in the human body, producing the largest rhythmic electromagnetic field of any of the body's organs. The heart's electrical field is about 60 times greater in amplitude than the electrical activity generated by the brain. This field, measured in the form of an electrocardiogram (ECG),

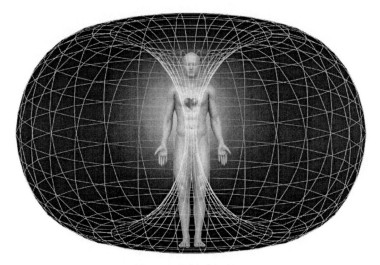

Magnetic Field of the Heart

can be detected anywhere on the surface of the body. Furthermore, the magnetic field produced by the heart is more than 5,000 times greater in strength than the field generated by the brain, and can be detected a number of feet away from the body, in all directions.[34] What is unique about the heart's electromagnetic field is that it is donut-shaped.

The communication between the heart and the brain is a dynamic, ongoing, two-way dialogue, with each organ continuously influencing the other's function. Research has shown that the heart communicates to the brain in four major ways:

1  Neurological communication – through the transmission of nerve impulses

2  Biochemical communication – via hormones and neurotransmitters

3  Biophysical communication – through pressure waves (pulse waves)

4  Energetic communication – through electromagnetic field interactions[35]

HeartMath Institute has carried out many experiments to investigate the intelligence of the heart. In one particular study called "Electrophysiological Evidence of Intuition: Part 1. The Surprising Role of The Heart", the researchers wanted to understand the roles of the heart and brain in intuition – a process of receiving information outside our conscious awareness. During the study they found that the body can respond to an emotionally arousing stimulus seconds before it is actually experienced. The study used 30 calm and 15 emotionally arousing pictures and these were presented to 26 participants. The participants were monitored for activity in the brain via an EEG (electroencephalogram) and activity in the heart using an ECG (electrocardiogram). What they discovered is that both the heart and the brain appeared to receive and respond to intuitive information seconds before the picture was shown, but the heart responded first. The heart would speed up if the picture to come was upsetting or shocking and it would slow down if the picture was calming. This study shows that surprisingly, the heart appears to receive and respond to intuitive information.[36]

In the second part of the same study called "Electrophysiological Evidence of Intuition: Part 2. A System-Wide Process", it was found that surprisingly, both the heart and the brain appear to receive and respond to intuitive information and even more surprisingly, there is compelling evidence that the heart appears to receive intuitive information seconds before the brain. This study also presents evidence that there is a gender difference in processing this information and it has shown that females are more attuned to intuitive information from the heart than men.[37]

This leads me to wonder if this is nature's way to ensure that mothers have the best possible chance of intuitively knowing how to keep their babies/children safe. When I was a baby, my mother left me in the garden sleeping in my pram. Suddenly, she got this strong feeling that something was wrong. She rushed into the garden to find that a tick (a small insect) had started to bury itself into my neck. The doctor afterwards told her that ticks often carry disease and it was good that she had caught it before it had attached itself.

### The Heart and the Reimprinting Process

Karl Dawson (the creator of Matrix Reimprinting) realised the importance of the heart field early on in his research, and heart pictures play a crucial role in the Matrix Reimprinting and Matrix Birth Reimprinting processes.

As we discussed earlier in the chapter on Matrix Reimprinting, when we experience a trauma, the information of the event is encapsulated as an image, which we subconsciously tune into over and over again until we get resolution on it. Part of the reimprinting process is to create a new picture, which rewrites the belief that we learnt about life in the moment that the trauma occurred, such as 'I'm not safe,' or 'People can't be trusted.'

To recap, Matrix Reimprinting rewrites that picture by giving a new experience to the part of you that created the old belief. This changes the belief in the subconscious and in your energetic field.

In Matrix Reimprinting, we use the heart to reimprint the new memory. We take the picture in through the top of the head first of all, to rewrite the neural connections in the brain. But it is the heart that sends the new picture out into the universe. The heart is the transmitter of the new information around the picture. These new pictures, sent out by the heart, are much stronger than the original pictures that we had. This is because positive pictures have a higher resonance than negative ones. The positive pictures engage higher emotional states such as empowerment, peace, joy, hope and freedom. These emotions have a higher resonance than fear, anger and despair. This is why, when we change a small number of these pictures for someone, dramatic healing can occur, because it is rewriting the field of the old event.

It is the heart's field that creates this dramatic shift, sending the new information out into the matrix.

### The Heart and Pregnancy

Joseph Chilton Pearce shares in his article, "Pregnancy, Birth and Bonding", that researchers at Whittlestone University in Australia found that the heart's field is essential for the connection between the infant and the mother. Pearce says, "The mother's heart has such a profound impact on the infant from the moment of conception on, that the system literally imprints to it on a cellular level; the entire neural system imprints to the mother's heartbeat."[38]

Pearce highlights that if you place a living heart cell in a petri dish, then the heart cell will beat a few times, go into defibrillation and die. But if you put two heart cells in the same petri dish, you will find that each heart cell will keep the other one going. They both entrain to each other and they end up helping each other keep beating. Each cell has its own electromagnetic field surrounding it, and when the two fields come into contact with each other, their waves entrain and go into the same coherent pattern, lifting both cells out of chaos into order.[39]

This is similar to what happens with the baby's heart as it connects to the mother's heart in the womb: the baby's heart develops and entrains with the mother's.[40]

Because of this entrainment, as soon as the baby is born, it needs to be placed within the mother's heart field space. Both the mother and baby benefit from this and they actually stabilise each other. If the mother has had a traumatic birth, by having her baby on her chest, her heartbeat will become more coherent. The baby's heart will also stabilise. This entrainment needs to continue for the first nine months until the baby's heart develops its own independent frequency. Any other caregiver, but especially the father and grandparents, can also help the baby's heart to stabilise in this way by having close contact.[41]

### The Heart and the Bonding Process
In the bonding process, the heart bonding time with the mother is essential. If there is no heart connection at birth because of separation from the mother, there can be severe distress for both the baby and the mother, and the baby can become withdrawn.

There is a 45-minute window after birth in which to establish the connection between the baby and mother. In that time, the baby's heartbeat entrains to the mother's. If entrainment does not occur, the baby's heart is compromised; heart disease can occur later in life because the heart has to work harder. Separation from the mother at birth can also lead to an underdevelopment of the nervous system and the heart-brain connection can be compromised.[42]

The bonding window doesn't just affect the baby. The mother is more likely to suffer from postnatal depression if her nurturing responses aren't activated in this way.

In one experiment by HeartMath Institute, newborn babies and their mothers were wired up to heart and brain recording devices (for ECGs and EEGs). These devices showed coherency and entrainment, i.e. the frequencies of the baby's heartbeat were reflected in the mother's brainwaves. Both the mother's heart and the baby's heart become incoherent if they are separated for a prolonged period of time.[43]

I have often wondered how much sudden infant death may correlate with this process. Sudden infant death (also known as cot death) usually occurs when the baby is in its cot. This usually means that the baby has been out of its mother's or father's heart field for a long period of time. From what I understand about the entrainment of the heart, it seems to me that in cases where the baby already had a weakened heart, perhaps its heart was not strong enough to keep beating by itself. This presents yet another valid reason for the mother to wear the baby in a sling and to have the baby close by in a cot by her bed at night.

Keeping premature babies in very close proximity to the mother's or father's body, with skin-to-skin contact, has been shown to save lives. What has affectionately come to be known as Kangaroo Care, because the mother and father spend 24 hours a day wearing their baby close to their bodies, has been shown to stabilise the baby's heart rate, regulate the baby's breathing and body temperature, promote longer sleep periods, improved feeding, more rapid brain development, more rapid overall growth and decreased crying.[44] My question is: if this is so beneficial to premature babies why do we not do this with full term babies too?

## Mother Restarts Heart of Baby
There is a famous case in Australia where a baby was not breathing when it was born.[45] The doctors tried to revive it, but to no avail. They gave the

mother her baby to hold so she could grieve. She held the baby on her chest, and spent somewhere between 20 minutes and half an hour stroking the baby and talking to it, with it held against her chest. Every now and then the baby would hiccup, almost as though it was taking a breath, before falling still again. The mother kept insisting, "Look, look, I think my baby's coming round." The doctors insisted that the baby was gone.

Eventually the baby came back to life. By being in the mother's heart field, and by being stimulated by the mother's stroking actions, it started breathing again and grew to be a healthy baby.

A baby can also stimulate the mother's heart. New mum Holli Cheung, 36, was left fighting for her life at Birmingham's Queen Elizabeth Hospital after she was struck down by acute myocarditis. She suffered a cardiac arrest and had to be resuscitated. Holli was put on a heart and lung machine to keep her heart going until doctors could work out how to treat her. One evening Holli's husband decided to leave their 3-month-old baby to sleep with her for a few hours and, to the astonishment of the doctors, her heart started to beat independently. When she could talk about it, Holli said, "I think for whatever reason, he woke up my heart."[46]

There is still so much to learn about the power of the heart and the electromagnetic field it creates. Some of the research from HeartMath Institute shows why the heart affects mental clarity, creativity, emotional balance and personal effectiveness. They offer techniques to help you shift your heart into 'heart coherence'; you can experience one for yourself in these 3 easy steps.[47]

### The Quick Coherence® Technique

#### Step 1: Heart Focus
Focus your attention on the area around your heart, the area in the centre of your chest. If you prefer, the first couple of times you try it, place your hand over the centre of your chest to help keep your attention in the heart area.

**Step 2: Heart Breathing**

Breathe deeply but normally and feel as if your breath is coming in and going out through your heart area. Continue breathing with ease until you find a natural inner rhythm that feels good to you.

**Step 3: Heart Feeling**

As you maintain your heart focus and heart breathing, activate a positive feeling. Recall a positive feeling, a time when you felt good inside, and try to re-experience the feeling. One of the easiest ways to generate a positive, heart-based feeling is to remember a special place you've been to or the love you feel for a close friend or family member or treasured pet. This is the most important step.

Quick Coherence® is especially useful when you start to feel a draining emotion such as frustration, irritation, anxiety or stress. Using Quick Coherence at the onset of less intense negative emotions can keep them from escalating into something worse. This technique is especially useful after you've had an emotional blow-up to bring yourself back into balance quickly.

## Heart Rhythm Patterns during Different Emotional States

The graphs below show examples of real-time heart rate variability (HRV) patterns (heart rhythms) recorded from individuals experiencing different emotions. The incoherent heart rhythm pattern shown in the top graph, characterised by its irregular, jagged waveform, is typical of stress and negative emotions such as anger, frustration, and anxiety. The bottom graph shows an example of the coherent heart rhythm pattern that is typically observed when an individual is experiencing a sustained positive emotion, such as appreciation, compassion, or love. The coherent pattern is characterised by its regular, sine-wave-like waveform. It is interesting to note that the overall amount of heart rate variability is actually the same in the two recordings shown; however, the patterns of

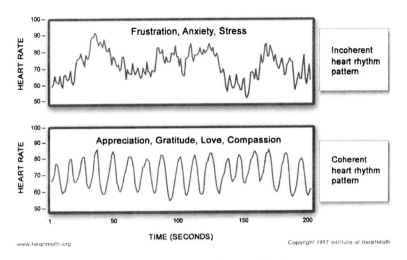

Heart Rhythms (Heart Rate Variability)

the HRV waveforms are clearly different.[48]

By maintaining the Quick Coherence technique and focusing on a positive emotion, the strength of the coherence or sine wave increases and not only has a greater effect on the body and mind, but also synchronises the heart patterns of those around you including your family, baby or pets.

One of the many experiments on heart rhythm entrainment that HeartMath Institute has carried out is with a boy called Josh and his dog Mabel. Both Josh and Mabel were fitted with a Holter (ECG) recorder and Mabel was placed in a room in one of their labs. Josh then entered the room and sat down and proceeded to consciously feel feelings of love towards Mabel. His heart rhythms became more coherent, and this change appeared to have influenced Mabel's heart rhythms, which then became more coherent. The study also showed that when Josh left the room, Mabel's heart rhythms became much more chaotic and incoherent, suggesting initial separation anxiety.[49]

The diagram below shows that Mabel's heart rate shifted into a more coherent state and changed back again when Josh left the room.

Putting the HeartMath coherence building techniques into

106

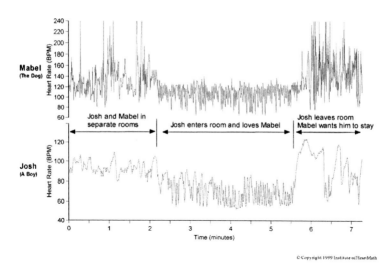

A Boy and His Dog (Heart Rhythms)

practice may help to entrain your baby's heart, whether in the womb or in the same room with you, and may also help to entrain all the other body organs to optimal efficiency. It can take the mother and the baby out of any fight-flight they might be experiencing and, as the mother self-regulates herself, her baby will learn how to self-regulate.

### Exercise
Take 10 minutes every day to practice the Quick Coherence® technique and send love and appreciation to your baby/child.

You can also imagine sending this love and appreciation back to your baby self, or any past younger part of yourself (ECHO) and indeed future part of yourself that is in need.

HeartMath Institute has very kindly given me permission to share their research. If you would like further information about any of these studies and others, go to www.heartmath.org.

In this chapter, we have touched briefly on the role of the heart, its innate intelligence, and its role in both the reimprinting and bonding process.

In the next chapter, we will look at the bonding process in more depth, exploring why it is essential for the connection between the mother and baby.

# Chapter 8

# The Importance of Bonding

*It is never too late to do the bonding process, as nature has designed it so the bonding process can happen at any time.* **Joseph Chilton Pearce**

In this chapter we will explore the bonding process, along with how some essential elements of this experience have been lost to the Western birthing paradigm. We will also highlight how the bonding process can be activated, even decades after the baby was born, with the Matrix Birth Reimprinting protocol.

Bonding is nature's way of ensuring the survival of the human race. There is one particular hormone that plays a vital role in bonding, and that is oxytocin.

## Oxytocin

Oxytocin is known as the love hormone. It is a neuropeptide made up of nine amino acids. It is made in the limbic brain in the area known as the hypothalamus and, according to scientist and bestselling author Dr David Hamilton, recent studies show that it is also made in the heart.[50]

Oxytocin and prostaglandins (a hormone-like lipid compound made in the placenta) help to stimulate the contractions in pregnant women at birth; they also soften the cervix and help with the placental separation and expulsion after birth.[51] Oxytocin also causes the release of milk from the mammary gland and levels rise when a mother touches her newborn baby. This hormone plays a pivotal role in creating the baby: it is there when we fall in love with our partners, have sex, and have orgasms. In fact, any connection to another person or something we love or have appreciation for, such as an animal, will trigger the release of oxytocin.

In their book *Orgasmic Birth*, Elizabeth Davis and Debra Pascali-Bonaro highlight that there is a link between oxytocin and theta brain waves.[52] This is the deepest level we can experience in a waking state. Theta is associated with extrasensory perception, creative inspiration, and spontaneous problem solving. It is also synonymous with being in heart coherence as we described in Chapter 7 and the natural brain state of the baby as we discussed in Chapter 4.

If the birthing and bonding processes are natural and unhindered, then the mother and the baby are completely entrained together: their heartbeats and breathing rhythms become synchronised, and the brain frequencies slow to theta. The birth can then progress naturally and easily. This entrainment can also affect everyone else in the room as long as they are loving, open and unafraid. In *What Babies Want* (DVD), Joseph Chilton Pearce describes his own experience of seeing his child being born, and how he was "stunned and surprised at the energy that filled the whole house," and that "the house shook with that energy." He goes on to say that it was "an awesome near-mystical experience and the closest thing to a wide-awake mystical experience, and to be present at a birth like that is an invitation to the greatest intimacy that life ever affords us, offered in just that moment. And it is the infant who is the one that offers that total vulnerable intimacy, and if we do not meet it, the infant feels betrayed by the world. They are coming into a world they cannot trust because it does not meet their most critical need at that point."

Fear or stress in the mother can block the production of oxytocin. The midwife, doula, doctor, nurse, OB/GYN or any other birth attendant can also unknowingly block the release of oxytocin during labour, if the mother begins to feel unsafe, feels like there is a lack of trust in her ability or she loses trust in the birth professional.

Oxytocin helps with the delivery of the baby and with the bonding process itself.

Oxytocin is also known as the shy hormone as it stops being produced if we feel like we are being watched or feel unsafe. For the mother, it is the hormone that helps her feel love for her baby. On a primal level, if the mother does not connect and experience the rush of overwhelming love in the moment of bonding, then she may not experience her instinct to nurture and protect the baby. That instinct needs to be triggered into action every time the baby cries and expresses a need. Without bonding, the triggering doesn't occur. Often mothers who don't have that release of oxytocin don't instinctively know what their baby needs or how to respond when their baby cries.

## Umbilical Cord
As we have mentioned before, it is important to leave the umbilical cord connected until it stops pulsing. This is usually between 10-20 minutes. And interestingly enough, the umbilical cord is 10-12 inches long, which means the baby can be held in Mum's arms with the cord still connected straight after birth.

## Bonding
During the first 45 minutes after birth, most babies are in an alert state, their eyes open in a bright, wide-eyed gaze, when the light in the room is not too bright.[53]

Nature has designed it so the baby can clearly focus only on objects up to 10-12 inches away. The main reason for this is so it can create an imprint of its mother's face when it makes eye-to-eye contact with her. This is why the baby is programmed to be more awake and aware; however, if anaesthetics or other drugs have been administered, the baby's consciousness will be affected. In a drug-free birth, the baby's inherent nature will lead it to search for its mother's face as soon as possible, so it can bond. The baby needs to be able to process its caregivers: 'OK, so you are my mother, and you are my father. These are the two faces that I need to connect with.' The baby ideally needs to be held skin-to-skin in its mother's arms (or the father's, if the mother is not available) and nurtured. The baby will be listening to its mother's and father's voices and will recognise them from the womb. It also gives it a chance to get used to its mother's smell and the feel of her body on the outside, as well as being held.

## Cingulate Gyrus

During the bonding process, the part of the brain called the cingulate gyrus, found in the mammalian part of the brain, is activated in both the mother and the baby. This part triggers the survival instincts for successful mothering. Once this part of the brain is activated in the mother, it connects with the prefrontal lobes (the civilised mind). It's the part of the mind that can feel empathy and compassion. The baby's prefrontal cortex begins to grow and neural pathways are created. This is the only part of the baby's brain whose development is not started in the womb; its development is very much experience-dependent at birth.

In the DVD, *What Babies Want*, which we mentioned previously, Joseph Chilton Pearce compares the activation of the cingulate gyrus to the awakening of an ancient wisdom. I see it as an intuitive opening that occurs and it connects us with the collective energy field of how to be a mother. It also connects the mother intuitively with her baby.

Even if the mother didn't have this experience when she was a baby, and didn't have that part of her brain stimulated by her own mother, as long as she is given the chance to bond with her own baby, the cingulate gyrus and the prefrontal cortex will still be stimulated.

The cingulate gyrus also connects with the heart, so when it is activated, the mother will literally feel her heart opening and the release of more oxytocin. For the baby, the neuro-structure connections of the heart and the connections to the emotional brain are either lost or made during the bonding process.

## Awakening the Cingulate Gyrus

Eye-to-eye contact between mother and baby is crucial for the awakening of the cingulate gyrus. But the mother looking at the baby in this way is not enough. The baby needs to *feel* nurtured. It is a complete sensory experience. Breastfeeding is part of this experience. So is

112

skin-to-skin contact and holding the baby. When the skin is stroked, the infant's nerve endings and the peripheral nervous system, which is an extension of the brain, are stimulated. In the womb, the baby's body is protected by the vernix (a waterproof coating of a fatty substance) so the nerves are not stimulated in the same way as they are after birth. Incidentally, the vernix also plays a vital role in breastfeeding and should not be washed off the baby, as it contains hormones that help to stimulate the baby to suckle.

Think about when an animal gives birth. Animals lick their young just after they are born. They may be cleaning them up, but they are also stimulating their offspring's sense of touch – it is the same for human babies. Touching, holding and stroking your newborn helps to stimulate the circulatory system. And for the parents, this opens up their primal sense of bonding. In the *What Babies Want* DVD, one father talks about his primal urge to lick his baby and another father talks about how the smell of the vernix burns itself into his lungs.

The baby also needs to smell the mother. A baby's sense of smell is heightened at birth. A baby can actually recognise the smell of its own mother's milk. In a scientific experiment, cotton wool pads were put over different mothers' breasts when they were producing milk. These pads were then presented to the babies. Each baby would only respond to its own mother's breast pad because that was the smell that it recognised.[54]

The baby also feels safe when it hears the mother's voice, which it recognises from the womb.

## The 45-Minute Window

As mentioned above, there is only a small window of opportunity to initiate the optimal bonding process at birth. In the DVD, *What Babies Want*, midwife Mary Jackson explains that in those first 45 minutes following birth, the bonding process is "like fresh glue" that enables the baby and mother to bond easily. When bonding takes place in this time period, the baby's body and brain is stimulated into bonding. Jackson explains that after the 45-minute time period, the "glue" starts to harden, and the mother and baby have to work harder to bond. All the physical and emotional development processes we have discussed thus take longer to be established.

Joseph Chilton Pearce states that if bonding doesn't take place in that time because the baby was separated from the mother at birth, it can still happen. When the mother is back with her baby, she can still make eye-to-eye contact and stimulate all the senses (as described above), initiating and completing the bonding process. However, because this does not occur within that optimal window of time, normal brain development can take up to three months longer to achieve.

Pearce also states that it is 'never too late' to experience this bonding process, no matter how old we are, as nature has designed it to keep this bonding option open and available to us at any time. This is why I believe the Matrix Birth Reimprinting process is so effective at healing our feelings of separation at birth, which we will discuss further on in this chapter and Chapter 9.

## If Bonding is Not Activated

So what happens if we don't have the bonding experience? In many cases it can lead to depression. When we are depressed, we often feel separate, isolated or alone. It makes sense that on a practical level, if bonding is not initiated, we will have the feeling that we are alone in the world, even if we are not. It is often an underlying feeling: one that we can't quite put our finger on. We don't know what is wrong with us. Something just doesn't feel right. These are the kinds of symptoms that are prevalent with babies who are born without bonding.

A lack of bonding can also create a host of beliefs about not being wanted. This can lead to subtle feelings of rejection. Anything in our external reality that triggers this feeling of rejection compounds our sense of separation.

Often babies who have not bonded are prone to substance abuse later in life, especially if the mother had drugs during the pregnancy or birth (something we will explore further in Chapter 10).

Change Agent Brett Moran is a recovered crack addict who had a profound spiritual awakening in the prison library when he was about to undertake a drug deal. Brett was a typical addict up until this point. He was addicted to everything – drugs, alcohol, sex, the Internet. After his awakening, Brett became a Change Agent, helping others to transform their addictive patterns and behaviours, and even starring in a film alongside Richard Branson, Desmond Tutu and Jack Canfield.

When Brett attended my Matrix Birth Reimprinting training, he shared how he was separated from his mother at birth and he never felt completely connected with her as a child. In his addiction work, he talks about how addicts often have what he calls 'a hole in the soul'. It is my belief that separation causes a hole in the soul, and we always try to fill that hole, which is where the addictive substances come in. They provide temporary relief but the hole is still there. The hole in the soul is a lack of love and we try to fill it with external things. We use alcohol, chocolate, food, drugs, online shopping, etc, but it is still there. We mistakenly believe that if we connect with something on the outside it will give us connection internally.

A similar thing can happen when a baby is put in an incubator and doesn't have human contact. The baby will actually bond with the incubator or the buzzing electric light strip above the incubator, simply because it is hardwired to bond.

I was teaching Matrix Birth Reimprinting on a workshop in Germany. I had my laptop and projector set up to present and, tripping over the cable, almost sent my computer crashing to the floor. One of the participants jumped out of his chair and caught my computer before it hit the floor. "I treat computers like they are my babies. I love anything technical," he told me. It was no surprise to learn that he was an incubator baby.

## Bonding and the Matrix Birth Reimprinting Process
Later on, when we learn Matrix Birth Reimprinting, you will discover how, even if bonding wasn't initiated at birth, you can still go back and do the bonding process, even decades after the birth. I've worked with clients in their eighties who didn't bond with their mothers at birth, who were able to initiate the bonding process. Pretty much everyone I have worked

with, from teenagers right the way through to adults in their later years, were profoundly affected by re-initiating the bonding process. Many reported that once they initiated the bonding process in the Matrix Birth Reimprinting sessions, their connection with their mothers, and with life in general, changed radically. This was the case whether their mothers were still alive or not.

We will explore more about how to use the Matrix Birth Reimprinting process for bonding in Chapter 12. It is one of the most fundamental aspects of the Matrix Birth Reimprinting process.

Now that we have explored the role of bonding in the birthing process, in the next part of the book we are going to look more deeply at the different kinds of birth traumas that are common in the Western birthing paradigm. A reminder: as we go into what might be considered some of the more challenging parts of this book, please remember that later you will learn a tool that will enable you to rewrite any traumas that you have experienced. If you are a practitioner who is working with clients with these issues, you will also learn many tools that will enable you to support them to release the birth trauma with Matrix Birth Reimprinting.

# Part 3

# Birth Traumas

# Chapter 9

# Separation at Birth

*There is a tremendous loss in human potential when birth becomes traumatic for the baby, mother and father…so many infancy and childhood problems are set in motion during the birth and bonding period…priority is to stop the harmful practice of separating mothers and their babies.* **Wendy Anne McCarty and Marti Glenn**

The following chapters will explore the different traumas that can occur in birth. Many of these traumas are a result of our Western birthing paradigm.

In the previous chapter, we explored the bonding process and the important role it plays in the relationship between mother and child. In this chapter, we'll explore the opposite of the bonding process, namely, separation, and the effects that can reverberate throughout life as a result.

Separation is a broad topic that affects a wide range of people on a multitude of levels, and isn't exclusive to the bonding process. The foundation of separation is the belief that we are alone in the world, unsafe and unloved. It is something that we are taught by the events that happen around our birth and in the first six years.

### Separated at Birth

The most common form of separation is when we are separated from our mother at birth. As babies we are totally helpless and depend on somebody else to take care of us. We are hardwired to believe that being separated from our mother is a potentially life-threatening situation.

This primal response can be activated in us at all times, even as adults. We are emotionally stronger and physically healthier when we are in a family setting or living in a community. This is why many of us crave connection and community. It even explains why social media such as Facebook is so popular. We are hardwired to belong.

I once carried out a session with a client from Russia. At the time that she was born, it was commonplace for babies to be put in a nursery for two weeks to enable the mothers to rest and recuperate after giving birth. This left my client with a lifetime of not being able to form close relationships and a feeling of being unloved and unwanted.

## Separation in the Womb

The hundreds of Matrix Birth Reimprinting sessions I have carried out have also taught me that babies can feel separate from their mothers in the womb. This occurs when the baby feels as though it is not wanted by the mother. It is also prevalent when the mother's heart is shut down and the baby cannot feel its mother's love for it. In the latter case, the baby also learns to close its heart to receiving love, as a way of protecting itself.

When I work with someone who is experiencing separation in the womb, they often believe that it was a mistake to come into this life, that they do not belong here and they want to go back to their source.

## Adoption

Adoption is one of the greatest sources of separation. The baby has known its mother energetically for nine months. It knows her sounds, her smell, and her vibration. Then it is born and given to somebody else. If the baby is given to somebody else straight from birth, then it may bond with the new mother. We are designed so that we can bond with those who we are first connected with. It is a survival mechanism that ensures the baby will live if the mother does not.

However, beyond bonding, adoption brings its own set of challenges.

Often, adopted children will go through life being highly compliant, moulding themselves into the person that their adoptive parents want them to be. Alternatively, they may swing in the opposite direction, continually testing their adoptive parents. Although they may not think it consciously, there is an element of, 'I'm going to push you, and push you, to see whether you will give me away.'

### 'Susie' – Adoption Case Study

Susie was adopted, and in her early twenties the adoption agency got in contact with her and told her that her birth parents wanted to connect with her. They lived in Ireland, a country where there are strict rules about termination and adoption. Susie's mother was unmarried and had had a relationship with a married man who couldn't leave his dying wife. After his wife died, they got together and married. They wanted to connect with Susie later in life. This put Susie in turmoil. She was bulimic, and the situation worsened her condition. She started to lose weight drastically.

Susie put everybody else before herself. She really felt like she was worthless because she had been given away. In all her relationships she would be constantly pleasing others. However, she always felt like she was failing at pleasing people, and that whatever she did was not enough.

In one of our sessions, we went back to the time when she was handed over to her adoptive parents. They turned up to take her just after she was born, but her birth mother didn't know whether she was doing the right thing and asked for more time to decide. She ended up keeping Susie for a week. It is easy to imagine that the birth mother would have been in turmoil, and that Susie would have picked up on the push-me-pull-me energy that the mother would have been experiencing, desperately wanting to keep her baby, but knowing that the society she lived in would have frowned on her bringing this baby home. In the end, she felt like she had no choice and that she had to give the baby up.

A week later, Susie was handed over to her adoptive parents. She says that they are two of the kindest people she has ever encountered. She loves them deeply. But when she was handed over to them she was still experiencing separation from her own mother.

After much debate, Susie did decide to meet her birth parents. Interestingly, she discovered that her mother was also bulimic.

During our session, all Susie was interested in was whether her birth mother and her adoptive parents felt OK. I had to press her to work on her baby self because the belief that she was not important was deeply ingrained in her. Much of our work together was enabling her to discover her self-worth.

## Mental and Emotional Issues

If somebody has experienced separation from their mother at birth, this can lead to patterns of depression in life. Depression can be a form of shutting down emotionally. It can lead to not being able to express your emotions, pressing your emotions down or not being able to be yourself. If a newborn baby is left to cry long enough, they will become exhausted and shut down and come to the belief that they are not wanted; they will feel isolated and alone. They are often angry but that anger remains unexpressed as nobody is there to hear them, feel them or see them. As we saw in Chapter 6, babies up to one year of age are functioning from their reptilian brain, i.e. they are only able to process the present moment in time. Their reptilian brain is focusing on survival, so if a baby is left to cry for a long period of time, to that baby it is a life and death situation. They do not have the cognitive ability to know that the last time they were left to cry, their mother came to them eventually. In this moment their mother/caregiver is not responding. This could mean abandonment and possible death, which leads to fear and repressed anger because their needs are not being met.

Separation at birth can lead to a wide range of emotional issues later in life, ranging from anxiety to severe mental and emotional disorders.

### 'Kirstie' – Birthed to Adoptive Mother

When Kirstie contacted me, she told me that she knew her adoptive parents were meant to be her real parents. She absolutely loved and adored her adoptive parents, but she wanted to feel an even closer connection with them. She asked me, "Will you carry out a Matrix Birth Reimprinting session with me so I can be born to my adoptive parents?"

My first thought was one of caution. I wasn't sure if it was ethical to do so. However, once I got past my thinking mind I could see her reasoning, so I agreed to carry out the session.

During the session, we cleared up some of the birth trauma that she instinctively knew she had experienced. Following that we went back and put her baby self into her adoptive mother's womb, guiding her through being born to her adoptive mum. When she had bonded with her adopted mother and father, I asked her, "How would it be if we brought your birth mother into the picture right now?"

"That would be great," she replied. She had no negative feelings towards her birth parent because she totally understood that she was meant to be with her adoptive parents. Her adoptive mother couldn't give birth, so she thanked the woman that had given birth to her for giving her life. Unexpectedly, she decided to bond with her birth mother too. This was the picture she reimprinted.

### Separation and Our Birth Stories

Although in this chapter we are focusing primarily on the way the birthing process impacts us on a physical level, and much of the rest of this book is focused on the emotional impact of our birth stories, it is also important to explore the effects of separation on our birth stories.

Right from the time of conception, all the way through to birth, we were connected to our mother, and in that period we didn't feel ourselves as separate from her. Even if we have a positive and supportive birth that incorporates all the elements, such as being born through the birth canal and keeping the cord attached, the moment we come out into the world, we no longer feel that connection to our mother. So it's really important that the mother help the baby experience that first moment of separation with as much care as possible. Having the mother hold the baby in her arms is the best way to ensure that the process of separation is eased for the baby. If you think about it, this is our first experience of connection in the outside world. And our first experiences of contact set up how we relate to the world in later life.

Now compare this to the many ways some Western medical establishments handle the birthing process. The baby is often pulled from the mother, and cleaned up before being handed back to her. The shock of that separation can be great for a newborn child.

In Chapter 4 on Matrix Reimprinting, we explored the kinds of traumas that cause what are known as a UDIN – a shock that causes a part of us to be frozen in time. A UDIN is one of the ways that an ECHO is formed. If you remember, a UDIN occurs when a situation is unexpected, dramatic, isolating, and there is no strategy to deal with it. Separation can cause a UDIN moment.

I had separation issues of my own when I was born. My mother was told that I was coming out too fast, so they gave her Pethidine to relax her and slow the labour down so she wouldn't tear. The Pethidine made her sleepy and she slept through most of the labour. When I was born, my mother held me for just a few minutes and then I was transferred to the nursery so she could sleep for four hours. So, like many people I work with, I had separation issues to clear.

## Suicide

Childhood and adult suicides are often linked to separation at birth. Also, if the baby has a near-death experience during the birth process, the child or adult can become fixated on the experience and often recreate it.

I recall listening to an interview with a child psychologist who talked about babies born with the cord around their necks. This, also, often leads to suicidal tendencies. He went on to say that if the child or adult chooses to commit suicide, it is usually by hanging themselves or some other form of asphyxiation like drowning. People who have sexual tendencies that involve getting to the point of suffocation before they can have an orgasm may have been born with the cord around their neck. It's almost as though they are trying to complete the process of not dying as a baby.

## Aggression and Violence

In Chapter 8 we discussed how, without the bonding process, the prefrontal cortex is not activated. Without the development of the prefrontal cortex, a person can be prone to a lack of empathy and compassion. When a child is separated from its mother at birth, feelings of anger and hatred can be created, which can show up in many forms later in life. Rape is one outlet. Rape is not usually about the sexual act, but rather about lashing out. For many men who rape, it is an expression of the anger and rage that they feel towards women. This can be triggered by separation from their mother at birth, and because they were emotionally neglected by their parents during childhood.

## Physical Manifestations of Separation Issues

Separation is not just an emotional issue. It becomes a physical issue too. In my experience, people who have experienced some form of separation either in the womb or at birth, either directly, such as losing a twin, or feeling separate from their mum before or after birth, are more likely to have eczema.-

In many cases, when I have worked through a separation issue with the mother, the child's eczema has resolved as a result. One client's 14-year-old son had eczema all up his spine. We worked on his birth and being separated from his mum at birth, and a year later his eczema had still not reappeared. A number of practitioners that I trained have also seen startling results with resolving birth separation issues with clients. Here is an example:

### 'Divya' – Eczema Case Study
### by Ted Wilmont, Matrix Reimprinting Trainer

A young professional Indian woman, Divya, came to see me. Her baby was a few months old and covered in eczema. When her baby was born, it was kept in the hospital for some time, and was given cortisol treatment. When Divya resisted the treatment for her baby, because she understood that the condition might be emotional in nature, she was told, "You're being a stupid bitch and you're endangering your child. It has to have this treatment."

We explored the issue of separation, but the baby had bonded with her at birth. I asked, "Did you suffer any separation during the pregnancy or just before it? Or did your husband or anybody connected with your baby suffer from that?"

She replied, "Yes, my grandfather died." Her grandfather lived in London and she had lived with him. They had been very close. She hadn't been allowed to go to the funeral or to the house to say goodbye because she's Hindu and a pregnant woman is not allowed to go to the funeral or to be at the house of the deceased, as it is believed that the soul of the deceased will be taken on by the unborn child.

We gave Divya the opportunity to say goodbye to her grandfather and worked on her anxiety about her child having eczema. We then reimprinted the birth. After this, the child's eczema started to clear.

## Asthma

In my experience, when the mother experiences some form of prolonged or unexpressed grief and sadness, such as when she loses a loved one whilst she is pregnant or before she is pregnant, her child may develop asthma. In Traditional Chinese Medicine (TCM), the lungs (and the skin) are linked to anxiety, sadness and grief. It is said that grief depresses and weakens the lungs and, like the effects of anxiety, it disturbs the easy and full movement of breath. Grief, of course, is also a form of separation, so children who have asthma often have eczema; it is reinforced if they are also separated from mother at birth.

## Negative Emotions Caused by Separation at Birth Include:
- Isolation
- Rejection
- Abandonment
- Anger
- Shame
- Fear

## Negative Beliefs Caused by Separation at Birth Include:
- The world is a dangerous place
- I'm not safe
- I'm not wanted
- People will always reject me
- I'm not good enough (especially in cases of adoption)
- I'm unlovable
- I'm unworthy
- I'm worthless
- I shouldn't be here

If you are experiencing any of those beliefs yourself, or you are a therapist working with clients, it is suggested that you go back to birth to see if the origin of them is in separation.

## Circumcision
Although male circumcision is not a trauma that happens during the birthing process, the procedure is usually carried out in American hospitals within 48 hours of birth. It causes severe trauma, separation from the mother, disruption of the bonding process and has lasting effects on the baby in terms of how he trusts the world around him.

Throughout the world, there are still some doctors who hold the

19th century belief that babies don't feel pain. Some doctors believe that if they do, it isn't an issue, because they do not have the brain development or capacity to remember traumatic or painful birth events. In fact, the opposite is true, as we mentioned previously. Babies have been found to have a significantly heightened level of sensitivity to pain following birth.

Babies do not have the emotional defence mechanisms to process their painful experience; it causes shock as well as physical pain and they can only deal with it by withdrawing and shutting down. When a baby is circumcised, he will scream wildly and try to escape. He is often restrained by being strapped to the table. Most often the freeze response will be activated: he will freeze and go into shock, increasing the risk of choking and breathing difficulties.

The University of Alberta 1997 study on circumcision found that all the subjects suffered pain, and some were traumatised to the point of danger. The study was halted prematurely after one of the subjects vomited, went into shock and stopped breathing for more than 25 seconds; the scientists realised just how traumatic the procedure was and couldn't carry on.[55]

Another study at Queens University in Ontario, in which babies' brain wave functions were monitored by fMRI and PET scanners, showed that the babies' brains were responding naturally up to the point of the first incision. Analysis of the MRI data after the first incision indicated that the surgery created a significant amount of trauma for the infants. The study showed changes to the limbic system, and particularly the amygdala (as we discussed in Chapter 6, the amygdala controls our emotional reactions, processes memory and is responsible for our decision-making).[56]

According to the neurologist who assessed the data, there was also a significant amount of damage in the areas of the brain relating to reasoning, perception and emotions. Follow-up tests indicated that the infants' brains never returned to their pre-surgery state, and that the damage inflicted by the circumcision was permanent.[57]

Psychologist Ronald Goldman, PhD testified at an historic

Parliamentary Assembly of the Council of Europe (PACE) hearing on January 28, 2014, stating that "Circumcision is a trauma." In his address, he highlighted how changes after circumcision include altered sleep patterns, extended crying, and disruptions in feeding and bonding. Infants may also withdraw after circumcision and be unable to communicate their needs. Circumcised infants still have increased pain responses six months after surgery. This can create neurological effects as severe as post-traumatic stress disorder (PTSD).[58]

Research shows that circumcised men are more likely to have erectile dysfunction, orgasm difficulties and premature ejaculation.[59] They are 4.5 times more likely to use erectile dysfunction drugs. Several medical societies recognise the long-term psychological effects of circumcision. Based on the collective responses of thousands of men, these effects include:
- anger toward parents and others
- sense of loss
- shame
- fear
- grief
- relationship difficulties
- depression
- sexual anxieties
- reduced emotional expression
- lack of empathy
- low self-esteem
- avoidance of intimacy

Goldman also reports that many circumcised men say that they wish they had been given a choice at a later time, rather than having it forced upon them when they were too young to resist.

There is often a lot of anger directed at their parents, along with a feeling of hopelessness, because the foreskin cannot grow back and the damage can never be undone.[60]

Goldman presents the long-term symptoms of circumcision,

which are synonymous with the pattern of PTSD. These include:
- avoidance of feelings and stimuli related to the trauma
- reduced emotional response
- a tendency to anger

It is said that the circumcision of his son re-enacts the father's unresolved traumatic emotional pain connected with his own circumcision, and allows the father to avoid confronting his emotional pain. Psychologists note that this compulsion to repeat the trauma is another classic PTSD symptom.[61]

Circumcision can also be traumatic for those in the medical profession to administer and to witness. In 2010 a trainee OB/GYN in America posted his account of witnessing a newborn baby having a circumcision on YouTube. It's clear from his description how conflicted he is about what he has just witnessed. He describes the event as follows: "The baby is strapped down because he is going to be kicking and fighting. It seems like it's torture for the baby but it's not because it is performed by a medical professional." He goes on to say how traumatic it is for the baby and painful for him as a man to watch. He describes how the baby screams and screams until he passes out, then wakes up and screams some more. The trainee then adds that he is still not sure if the baby is feeling anything.

After filming the video, the trainee put this follow-up account underneath the video on YouTube called "What Happened Today".

As a medical student at America's oldest hospital, Pennsylvania Hospital, I was happy to be on the obstetrics rotation. While still in college, I had heard an obstetrician speak enthusiastically about his optimistic specialty. So now I was enjoying helping to bring babies into the world. While professors provided good background information in formal lectures, my real teachers were residents only a few years older than I was. They took turns talking me through normal deliveries.

Almost every doctor can recall the joy of delivering a healthy normal infant. This joy was shattered one day when one of the residents said, 'There are some circumcisions that need to be done, go and do them.' At the time I guess I knew what a circumcision was, but that was about it. I had certainly learned nothing about the subject in medical school. Obediently, I proceeded to the newborn nursery, where another medical student was already waiting. I felt nervous, and he looked quite nervous, too. Strapped to a board on the long counter in front of each of us was a bawling male infant. Beside the infant was a surgical tray filled with instruments. Imagine our consternation when we found there was no one to tell us what to do. Obediently, we put on surgical gowns, then surgical gloves. Then we began to try to figure out how to use what I later learned was a Gomco Clamp.

As far as I know, I made a fairly neat job of it. But my abiding memory of that day is of my colleague. He was one of the more brilliant members of our class, and was planning to become a radiologist. As for surgery, forget it. He was all thumbs. I still remember him, standing beside me, fumbling with the complicated instruments, proceeding to use them on the helpless penis before him, all the while just shaking his head!

I look back on the only time I have ever performed any circumcisions with regret and resentment. I resent having had no opportunity to study circumcision in medical school or to consider whether I thought it a treatment for anything. I resent the resident commanding me to do it, while offering no further guidance or help. In fact, I was treated just as the medical profession treats innocent new parents today. Doctors tell them a circumcision needs to be done. Before the new parent has time to consider, it is all over. Then it is too late to say no, and everyone has to live with the consequences. I was a medical student, so a lot of the responsibility was mine. I clearly violated, all in one instant, the Golden Rule (I certainly would not have wanted that done to me), the major tenet of medical practice, First, Do No Harm, and all seven principles of the American Medical Association's Code of Ethics. Mind you, I did not realise it then, just as unwary medical students do not realise it today. Now I know there are no valid medical indications for routine neonatal circumcision. I realise much harm can be done, evidenced by the thousands of men who have written their testimony and who have told me personally of the harm done to them. Now I also realise that I violated my patient's basic human right to enjoy his entire body intact, while all he could do was scream his tiny head off. That was some years ago, but it might just as well have been last year.

The United States is the only country in the world that, for no religious reason, severs part of the penis from the majority of its newborn males. I speak out in the hope that many parents and doctors will read this before getting swept into the cultural madness of routine neonatal circumcision. What should one do if called upon to consent to or to perform circumcisions? Just say NO! In so doing, you will be taking the only ethical position there is on this issue.[62]

Like many of the core issues in our Western medical model that are asking to be transformed, we can only make a change if people are aware of the impact of the issue. It is my hope that we collectively take a stand against this barbaric procedure, and the first step towards making a change is increasing awareness about the issue.

**Exercise**

If you find that this section has brought up a lot of emotions around separation or circumcision, you can follow these simple steps:

1 Sit with your hand on your heart and breathe in for the count of 5 and out for the count of 5.
2 Start tapping on your finger points or another tapping point that feels good to you.
3 Identify in your body where you are feeling the disruption in energy (throat, heart, solar plexus, stomach, etc.).
4 Focus on that energy disruption. If it had a colour to it, what would it be? (red, yellow, black, etc.)
5 What emotion would be in that coloured energy?
6 What colour would you need to bring in to lift and lighten that energy/emotion?

7 Now send that healing colour back through your past to where this feeling was first created. This may be in the womb, at birth or as a baby left alone in their cot or even later on in childhood.

8 Get a sense of yourself at that time being wrapped in that coloured energy safety blanket and keep tapping on your fingers or your chosen point.

If you are short on time, then often this is enough to start to lift the energy from your body and make you comfortable until you can work more on this memory or until you find a therapist to work with.

If you want to go deeper with this exercise, carry out the following steps:

9 Imagine stepping into the picture with your baby self in the womb, your newborn self or your older baby self.

10 What is the first thing you are sensing about your younger self?

11 Ask her/him what they need to help them here. Some options are:

   a) Tap on your baby self for the emotions they are feeling. Example: 'Even though you are feeling scared and alone, you're safe right now, I'm here.' Tap around the points on feeling scared and alone.

   b) Talk with them and let them know they are not alone and that you are there to help them.

   c) Once the energy of the emotion has lifted, ask them if they would like somebody else to come into the picture here – i.e. their mother or father, an angel, an animal…Or maybe they are just happy that you are there with them.

   d) Find out from them what decision they made about

life and themselves at that time. It may be that this is where they decided they were unlovable or that the world was not safe.

12 With your knowledge and understanding, help them to discover the truth of what is really happening here.

13 What would be a new, more positive belief they would like to feel and what needs to happen in order for that belief to be created? Maybe they need to be reunited with mother or they need you to hold them to help them feel safe.

14 Finish either with a full reimprinting of the picture (as below) if you feel you have reached a really positive place, or if you feel there is more work to do at another time, just hold the picture of your baby self surrounded in a protective coloured energy blanket in your heart until you can come back and work again.

**Reimprinting Process**

1 See your baby self in that picture and list the positive emotions and beliefs that are there, i.e. I'm safe, loved and protected.

2 Notice a beautiful colour coming from, and surrounding, this picture.

3 Take the picture into your mind and allow your mind to reconnect with that new way of feeling and that new way of being.

4 Send the energy around your body.

5 Take the picture into your heart and allow your heart to fill with the colour you have chosen.

6 Open your heart and send the colour and the emotions out to every cell in your body.

7 Open your heart again and send the picture out into the universe on a beautiful, coloured ray of your choice.

8 Allow the universe to send you back even more of that coloured energy.

9 Finish by taking a few deep breaths.

Having explored separation and the Western birthing paradigm in this chapter, including the related trauma of circumcision, in the chapter that follows we will begin to look at the effects of drugs on our birth stories.

# Chapter 10

# The Use of Drugs during Labour

*Over 90% of all infants in the U.S. are born with drugs (e.g. narcotics from epidurals, Pitocin, Acetaminophen, etc.) in their systems. None of these drugs have been tested for safe use in infants.* **Catherine Beier**

With the evolution of Western medicine, a whole host of drugs has become normalised in childbirth. If we take a moment to step back and think about this logically, it makes no sense to drug a tiny being as it comes into the world. The fact that we routinely use drugs in the birthing process is synonymous with our lack of understanding about the consciousness of the baby, which we explored in Chapter 2. If we understand the baby as a conscious being, then drugging them to enter the world becomes a barbaric practice, or at least one that should be only entered into when there are no other alternatives, and when the life of the mother or baby is in danger. With this in mind, we will explore the impact of Western medicine on the birthing process.

### The Road to Medical Intervention
As we discovered in Chapter 8, if the mother goes into fear, labour can stop. It can also stop due to the use of drugs. In many hospitals there is a rush for the birthing process to happen, so if labour is not moving along as it should or it is not progressing fast enough, then Pitocin will be administered to the mother, making the contractions stronger, faster and more painful for her. This intense pain becomes unbearable, so the mother is then given an epidural, which numbs the pelvis but makes

the birthing process slow down again or stop, so more Pitocin is given to speed things up again. The baby in the womb is experiencing these very intense and strong contractions that can compromise its oxygen supply, so this then becomes an emergency situation. The mother is advised her baby is at risk and that she needs a C-section. What starts out as something to help the mother and baby along, quickly develops into an emergency situation and major surgery.

What also hinders the birth process is the fact that the mother is lying on her back at the end stages of labour. When she is on her back, the pelvis becomes narrower and it is more difficult for the mother to use her stomach muscles to push. For the baby, it is more difficult to navigate through the narrow pelvis, but also more difficult to make the turn it needs to get its body around the different angles of the pelvis. This leads to an increased risk that the baby will get stuck and if that does happen, the mother will either need an episiotomy (a surgical incision of the perineum and the posterior vaginal wall, making the opening larger for the baby to come out) and/or ventouse suction cup or forceps will need to be used. Mothers who squat, or sit on a birthing stool, find it much easier to birth their baby, as they have gravity to assist them and also they can move their bodies around in a circular motion to assist the baby to navigate through the pelvis.

**Exercise**

If you are in a safe position to do so, and squatting is easy for you, please stand up and follow these instructions.

- Place the index finger from your left hand on your coccyx (your tailbone at the bottom of your spine).
- Place the index finger from your right hand on your pubis at the front of your body opposite the tailbone.
- Notice the distance between your fingers.
- Gently squat down and as you do notice what happens to the pelvis and the gap between your two fingers.
- Stand back up and gently tilt backwards slightly as if you are lying down on a bed. Again notice what happens to the space between your fingers and what happens to your pelvis.

**Exercise by Debra Pascali-Bonaro**

What you will notice doing this exercise is that your pelvis opens up when you squat and closes up more when you're in a lying position. In the Western world, having women give birth lying on their backs was introduced for the convenience of the medical profession and not as an aid to the baby or the labouring mother.

We will explore the physical and psychological effects of these damaging types of birth experiences throughout this chapter and Chapter 11.

## Anaesthetic Birth

Statement from World Health Organisation (1984):

> Some obstetric techniques which involve giving drugs have become virtually routine in certain centres or countries; the fact that they are much less widely used elsewhere shows that they are not essential to normal delivery. No form of drug therapy should be used in delivery except where there is a specific indication for it.[63]

The use of anaesthetics in births is a common practice in the West. Yet anaesthetics can create a UDIN moment for the baby. Not only are they frozen in shock because they experienced the anaesthetic unexpectedly, but they often will hold the anaesthetic within their bodies. This means that they are frozen on two levels – emotionally and physically.

The baby always receives an overdose. This is because the anaesthetic is administered according to the mother's body weight. When it is born, the baby has a high percentage of fat cells, and the anaesthetic is held in these fat cells. It is said that it takes the baby up to three weeks to eliminate 95% of the drug from their body.[64]

A commonly used pain relief drug called Pethidine is a narcotic that is administered by intramuscular injection to the mother. It takes up to 20 minutes to work for the mother, but it easily travels to the baby via the placenta. Before the birth, the mother's liver processes the drug; however, if the baby is born within one hour following administration, then the baby's immature liver struggles to process the drug left in its body. Research has also shown that if Pethidine is given two to three hours before birth, it is likely to cause breathing difficulties; the higher the dose the mother receives, the greater the effect it has on the baby.[65]

The effects of Pethidine on the baby directly after birth are drowsiness and the baby is unresponsive; and it is the drug most known for inhibiting breastfeeding. If the baby does breastfeed, then the mother can unkn-owingly give the baby a second hit of the drug through the breast milk.[66] Over the long term, the baby is more likely to cry for long periods of time.[67]

I have done countless sessions of Matrix Birth Reimprinting with adult clients whose mothers received anaesthetics at birth, and when we release the emotional shock that was created at that moment, many times I have actually smelt the anaesthetic on their breath as it is released from their body. However old someone is, the anaesthetic is held in their fat cells until the shock is released. When we release the shock with Matrix Birth Reimprinting, the body is able to release the anaesthetic simultaneously.

An anaesthetic birth usually takes place when something has not gone to plan. This means that the mother herself is likely to already be in shock, fear or trauma. The baby will be registering this. The addition of anaesthesia creates a double shock for the baby – first they are picking up the mother's stress, and the anaesthetic added on top of that heightens the trauma response.

When a child is delivered without anaesthetic, it goes through a natural bonding process, which we explored in Chapter 8. Paediatrician Dr Lennart Righard and Margaret Alade, a midwife,[68] studied two groups of newborn babies. In one group were mothers who had no medication during labour and in the other group, mothers who had medication during labour. All the babies were placed on the mothers' bellies, and from there, they could crawl up to the breast. This is a natural reflex for a newborn. However, all the babies that had been anaesthetised were too drugged to be able to make this journey. You can see a video of this in the membership site details at the end of this book.

As we highlighted in Chapter 8, one of the most vital elements of the bonding process is when the mother and baby make eye contact for the first time. A baby who has been drugged at birth will not be alert enough to make eye contact with its mother. Not only does this affect the bonding process, but it can lead to other difficulties. The immediate consequences for the baby include:
- challenges with breast feeding
- newborn trauma crying (the baby keeps crying continuously)
- reduced level of awareness

The longer-term effects of an anaesthetic birth include lingering emotions such as:
- fear
- shock
- overwhelm
- feeling out of control
- terror
- anger
- rage
- resentment
- helplessness
- powerlessness[40]

These emotions are often generated because the baby's instinct, which is to be born naturally and without drugs, has been bypassed. When this happens, there is likely to be an underlying sense that something was taken away from them. They have no conscious reasoning through which to express and process this experience, so they end up with a sense of anger, helplessness and powerlessness. Have you ever had an experience where you were doing something and someone came in and took over? How did you feel? It's the same for the baby. This is what causes anger, rage and resentment. The sense that 'I could have done this on my own,' is very strong.

Adults who had an anaesthetic birth also tend to be anxious about upcoming events because of their lack of confidence in themselves about whether or not they know enough. They might find themselves in situations where they feel like they've got it under control and then all of a sudden something unexpected happens and they lose confidence, mirroring what happened in the birth. They might start a project, feel confident at the beginning and suddenly get triggered into 'I don't know enough' and go into a paralysed state.[70]

In my work with Matrix Birth Reimprinting, I have seen many cases where the lingering effects of anaesthesia affect children and adults, years or even decades after they were born. Anaesthesia can create a general loss of awareness. Often those who have had anaesthetic births report that they feel spaced out when challenges or difficulties arise in life. They can find themselves checking out, or freezing and waiting for somebody else to help them get out of the situation they are in, because this is what was modelled to them in the birthing process. It is common for children who experienced births of this nature to seem like they are present one moment and absent the next.

In the Matrix Birth Reimprinting protocol, which we will explore further in Chapter 12, I take clients back to the memory of being in the womb. This memory is stored in the subconscious mind and the Matrix Birth Reimprinting protocol enables us to access what occurred.

### 'Roger' – Anaesthetic Birth

I carried out this process with Roger, who had experienced an anaesthetic birth. When we took him back to his memory of being in the womb, it was hazy. He could see his mother's pregnant belly, but he couldn't connect with her as a complete being. The reason he could only see her belly was because she was unconscious when he was born, so his mind had created a metaphor for her absence. I worked with Roger for three sessions. First, our work was centred around releasing the anaesthetic from his mother. We then focused on him as a baby, helping him to release the anaesthetic from his own body. When we had done so, he had a full view of his mother's body, including her head, arms and legs.

It is interesting to note that in many cases a birth trauma can be cleared in a single session. I have noticed on numerous occasions that anaesthetic births can take more time to clear, because we are dealing with the effects of an intoxicating drug on the system of an infant, and the impact of the anaesthetic often seems to go deep.

## Epidurals

Epidurals are also a form of anaesthetic. As soon as you administer an epidural, it switches off most of the natural birthing hormones. Due to the loss of feeling that the epidural creates, the natural birthing process can either slow down or stop. This can often result in a C-section. An epidural often lowers the mother's blood pressure and sometimes gives both the mother and baby a fever.[71] In the USA, when a baby is born with a fever, the first thing the doctor will do is give it antibiotics. Even though it is known that epidurals cause fever, antibiotics are administered as a safety precaution. This means that the baby coming into the world has the shock of the epidural, a fever as a consequence, and then is administered antibiotics that it doesn't need. Its gut flora (bacteria in the gut that aids digestion), which is just beginning to develop, is wiped out with antibiotics, which usually leads to indigestion and colic.

Epidurals slow down the progress of labour. The body-brain connection is lost, slowing the natural progression of the baby down the birth canal which is why a C-section is often required.

The epidural can also give the baby a numb mouth, which can hinder breastfeeding. Epidurals interfere with the release of oxytocin, which not only will affect the mother's ability to produce milk, but can also hinder the bonding process.[72]

It takes approximately 3 or 4 minutes for the baby to actually receive the anaesthetic. So if a C-section has been agreed upon, and they give the mum the epidural and then go straight into the operation, the baby may not have received the anaesthetic yet and might still be 'conscious'. The same thing can occur with a forceps delivery. If the baby has not yet received the anaesthetic it can cause pain as a result (we will explore instrument delivery further in the next chapter).

A baby who has been born with an epidural can have a tendency to be 'lost' later in life. Something occurs and, as an adult, they just go into a kind of vagueness, similar to that of an anaesthetic birth. It's as though all their inner knowing shuts down. If you have ever been triggered into fight or flight, you will know that in that moment, your reasoning process stops. As we highlighted in Chapter 6, flight or flight triggers the reptilian brain. The most common example of this is when we go into an exam room and suddenly we can't think of the answers that we knew five minutes ago. A similar thing happens to a baby who has had an epidural or other type of anaesthetic birth. It often creates a sense that life is being put on hold (which it was during the birth, if you think about it metaphorically). They can also end up putting someone else's pain, fear and needs before their own later in life, which is again a metaphor for what happened to them at birth. Often it can create a belief that they are not important, or that everybody else is more important than they are.[73]

William Emerson shares a case study of a nurse who was trying to resolve her birth trauma through the work she chose to do by confronting the trauma and trying to find a solution. I also believe that we often choose our birth experience so we can fulfil part of our life purpose.

She was anesthetized during birth and lost consciousness. As an adult, she was an avid teacher of consciousness-raising techniques, teaching her students to remain aware during life's most stressful and difficult moments. She also promoted drug-free births and taught medical personnel to be in touch with their vital energies, so that they would be able to avoid medical burnout, which she defined as being numb, out of touch, and unfeeling when treating patients in medical situations.[74]

## Drug Addiction

The use of drugs during labour or during pregnancy can also be linked to drug addictions later in life. A study by six senior doctors, led by Dr Bertil Jacobson at the Karolinska Institute in Stockholm, examined increased rates of suicide in young people and the correlation with deaths from cirrhosis of the liver. Birth record data were gathered for 412 forensic victims comprising suicides, alcoholics and drug addicts born in Stockholm after 1940, and who died there during the years 1978-1984. These were compared with 2,901 controls. The researchers looked at the pain relief policies of the hospitals in which the subjects had been born.

The results were alarming. There was a correlation between birth trauma and later suicide by mechanical means. For example, those who committed suicide by hanging, strangulation or drowning were four times as likely as the controls to have suffered asphyxiation during birth. Mothers of those who died from drug overdoses were twice as likely as controls to have had opiates in labour, and three times as likely to have been given barbiturates.

They even found that babies born in certain hospitals were more prone to addictive behaviours than those born elsewhere. For example, 14% of the babies were born at one hospital, but it accounted for 27% of the addicts. The hospitals which had used more nitrous oxide (more commonly known as gas and air) produced more addicts. After testing for other variables, the authors found that being born at one hospital increased the risk of later amphetamine addiction by 3.7 times.

When addicts' births were compared with those of their siblings, it was more likely that, for theirs, nitrous oxide was administered for pain relief in labour, and for longer periods. The longer the exposure to nitrous oxide in utero, the greater the risk of later addiction.[75]

In *The Afterlife of Billy Fingers*, Annie Kagan, sharing information from the afterlife after her brother had passed, gives us an insight into how his addiction patterns were created:

> Although in my younger days Mommy was always the one who bailed me out of trouble, our relationship was difficult from the day I was born. That's the thing about human beings. They're not just one side of the coin.
>
> Actually the whole thing between Mommy and me started even before I was born. Soon after Mommy got pregnant with me, she started to bleed. She bled so much she began thinking I was trying to kill her from inside her womb. So she developed this kill-the-baby-before-he-kills-you kind of attitude.
>
> The doctors prescribed bed rest – complete bed rest and injections to calm her down. In those days, they didn't know that it wasn't so great to give a pregnant woman morphine. Morphine can make unborn babies develop a taste for it. So you could say I was getting high back there in the womb.[76]

It was interesting that not only did he receive the morphine but also the belief that his mother thought he was trying to kill her from inside the womb. This obviously impacted him later in life.

## Toxic Womb

My personal in-womb trauma came from being in a toxic womb – my mother smoked throughout her pregnancy as many mothers did in the 1960s. I discovered why I had such an aversion to cigarette smoke when I was delivering a Matrix Birth Reimprinting training in Prague. At that time, smoking was permitted in the restaurants and pubs within the city. I used to be a smoker. I smoked between the ages of 13 and 26 and when I gave up I became an avid anti-smoker. I found that I disliked cigarette smoke intensely. Also, vehicle exhaust fumes bothered me.

When we were out in Prague, I experienced an emotional trigger from the smoke.

A lot of the restaurants in Prague are tucked away in back rooms without ventilation, and we were eating in one of them. At one point when everyone around me was smoking, I went into flight. "I've got to get out of here!" I said, running out of the room. I found a spot in a busy, but relatively smoke-free, corridor. I imagined tapping on myself. *Why is this affecting me so much?* I asked myself. *What does it remind me of?* I had a sudden realisation that it reminded me of being trapped in the womb. I had a session booked with Sasha Allenby (co-author of *Matrix Reimprinting Using EFT*) the following week and we were going to do a trade session around our births, although up until that point, my understanding was that my birth was uneventful. It hadn't been in my awareness that my mother's womb had been toxic because she smoked. Just knowing that we were going to resolve this in a week's time was enough to release the trigger enough for me to re-join the course participants at dinner.

The following week when I got together with Sasha, I asked her what she knew about her birth (before I revealed what had happened the week before). She said, "My mum smoked and drank when I was in the womb; I feel like it was a toxic environment." It was obvious at that point why we had paired up to resolve this theme.

In the 1960s and '70s, cigarette smoking during pregnancy wasn't frowned upon, so both our mums were doing the best they could with the knowledge and wisdom that they had.

We both went back and cleared our toxic wombs during that session. When Sasha said to me, "Where do we need to start with yours?" I replied, "We need to start with me in Prague last week." As I did, I got the sudden realisation that when I had done imaginary tapping on myself the week before in Prague, I had felt better so quickly, because my future self from this session I was doing with Sasha had travelled back in time to help me! In that moment I got a profound understanding of timelessness, and how when we do this work, we are working on a quantum level where there is no past or future, and where everything exists all at once. The other interesting thing that happened two months after the session was that my mother gave up smoking. During the session, I had brought Brett Moran into the picture

146

to help my mother with her addiction to cigarettes.

I cleared my mum's toxic womb in that session. There was still some work to do around toxic breast milk because my mum smoked whilst breastfeeding and as a child I used to eat cigarettes. (I guess I was craving the nicotine.)

Sasha cleared her mum's toxic womb too. Sasha's pregnant mum had shared a bottle of alcohol with two friends the night before she was born (which was not an unusual practice in the '70s in Northern England). As a result, Sasha came into the world intoxicated. It is no surprise that in her twenties she was a drug addict and an alcoholic.

As an aside, the first words Sasha ever heard were: "Look at the mess you made." Her mum had been left with an inexperienced trainee midwife who had told her to push too soon. The qualified midwife had come through after Sasha had been born. Her mother had split, and the midwife scolded her for splitting. But as these were the first words that Sasha ever heard, she integrated them as truth, and then had to work hard to overcome her messy and chaotic patterns as a child and later in life. These words obviously reverberated for her on a subconscious level long after she was born.

## The Effect of Drugs on the Mother

Mothers who give birth with the intervention of drugs often feel like they have missed out on something. The use of drugs during birth often leaves the mother feeling unfulfilled, or as though she has lost something. Often she feels as though she has failed somehow, because her body didn't respond as it should have done. If the decision to use drugs was taken out of her hands, she may have been left with a sense of anger because the opportunity for a natural childbirth had been taken away from her. Many mothers I have worked with expressed the emotion of 'grief', as it felt like they were grieving the natural birth experience that they had planned. As we discussed earlier, mothers who were unconscious at the time of the birth miss out on the initial bonding process, and the baby can feel abandoned by the mother as she was emotionally unavailable at this crucial time.

## Induction and Augmentation

Induction is the process by which labour is started using Pitocin, the synthetic version of oxytocin. In addition, the amniotic sac is artificially ruptured to break the waters.

Augmentation is the administration of drugs to speed up a labour that has already started.

The following information was taken from William Emerson's article, "Birth Trauma: The Psychological Effects of Obstetrical Interventions":

> Back in 1994, researcher Shanley said that between 20% and 40% of all US hospital births involved the use of drugs such as Pitocin. That is a huge percentage of babies born under the influence of these drugs.[77]

Induction and augmentation lead to shock, feeling invaded, bonding difficulties, and can lead to drug addiction later in life as we mentioned earlier.[78]

One of the obvious side effects of piercing the amniotic sac is boundary issues. This includes not being able to either set one's own boundaries or respect other people's boundaries.

Induction and augmentation can also lead to rescuer issues for the child or adult. This can include starting something and needing rescuing when it gets tricky, or getting angry if someone tries to rescue them.[79]

Self-esteem issues are also prevalent among this group – they have a sense that they can't do things themselves. Resentment and loss of control are common among this group. Often when they are triggered, they will talk really fast or do something irrational in order to regain control of the situation. They may give out a message that they do not know how to get started and thus need inducement from others. They may also let others decide for them because they think they don't have what it takes to know their own way in life.[51]

These kinds of births lead to the circulation of higher levels of adrenaline in the body. They set the stage for the HPA (hypothalamus, pituitary, adrenal) axis to be more readily triggered, and create an elevated sense of stress, attack and danger.

---

**Lee Ann – Transforming a Traumatic C-section Experience**

Lee Ann experienced a traumatic birth with her first child. With her second child she experienced an empowered birth.

Lee Ann was pregnant with her second child and began working with me two weeks before she was due to give birth. She initially contacted me because she and her husband were experiencing a high degree of fear around giving birth to their second child because the first birth had been so traumatic. She was clear that for this birth, she wanted to have a natural experience. She had taken steps to educate herself on how a natural birth should be, and had also found an obstetrician who had a great record of VBAC births (vaginal birth after caesarean). In addition, she had hired a doula to help her through the labour. However, she was still experiencing the fear of the birth process itself.

Lee Ann shared the story of her first birth with me. Labour had been induced by Pitocin. She had been given an epidural, but it hadn't worked effectively and her pelvis wasn't numb, so she could still feel all the contractions. She then went on to have an emergency C-section and when they cut her open she could feel everything they were doing to her.

In our first two sessions of Matrix Birth Reimprinting, we cleared all the trauma that had led up to the C-section, including the induced labour and the epidural, the feeling of powerlessness and being out of control, and also how she had felt when she was not being listened to.

Our third session via Skype took an unexpected turn. "You'll never guess what. My waters have broken, my mucus plug is coming away, I can feel the starting of contractions and I'm so happy because I didn't get to feel this last time because they induced me."

149

"OK, so you're going to have the baby very soon. We really do need to clear the trauma of the C-section and if we've got time, we'll do a future reimprint as well," I told her.

In this third session we helped Lee Ann to get her power back. We cleared the shock of being cut open. She recalled how she had been determined to make sure her baby was OK before she allowed them to anaesthetise her completely. She heard her baby crying and the anaesthetist had said, "She is going into cardiac arrest: I have to put her under." That was the last thing she heard. We tapped on her ECHO to clear all the pain, shock and fear. We also tapped on her baby, Lyla, in the picture, to help her feel safe and release any fear she may have been holding.

We also worked surrogately with her husband Joel (in other words, we worked on his behalf when he was not there). I had actually been scheduled to work with Joel the following day but for obvious reasons this was not going to be possible, so we decided to include Joel in the session with Lee Ann working surrogately on him. We cleared Joel's shock of seeing his wife in so much pain. We also cleared the fear he had when his wife was operated on. Particularly strong for him was the fear of losing both Lee Ann and their unborn child. (For Joel's full session see Chapter 18.)

One of Lee Ann's biggest regrets was that she was unconscious for the first two hours of Lyla's life, and although Lyla was in her father's arms during this time, Lee Ann felt she had missed out. Because of the imminent birth, after we had cleared the trauma of the C-section, there was no time to guide her back through a natural birth as I normally would have. Instead, she bonded with Lyla and we reimprinted that picture.

As her new baby, Mia, was about to arrive, we carried out a future Matrix Birth Reimprinting session with her. Lee Ann connected with the baby and I guided her to show Mia how the natural birth was going to be. She was instructed to see herself giving birth and to bring in her colour for empowerment. She chose yellow. We imprinted the picture of Lee Ann bonding with Mia.

Lee Ann went on to have a very natural birth with Mia and a textbook bonding experience, just as we had imprinted. Later she shared with me how she held that picture in her mind of the future birth imprinting and how the energy, emotions and colour of the imprinting session helped her stay strong and focused throughout the labour.

(You can view the recording of this session at the membership site. Details at the back of this book.)

Now that we have explored some of the consequences of drug-induced births, in the following chapter we will consider the effects of instrument delivery on the mother and baby.

# Chapter 11

# Instrument Delivery

*It is important to keep in mind that our bodies must work pretty well, or there wouldn't be so many humans on the planet.* **Ina May Gaskin**

In the last chapter we explored the effects of drugs on childbirth. But it isn't just medication that affects our belief systems and sense of self. Instrument deliveries also have a profound effect on the baby, and these include C-section, forceps delivery and vacuum extraction.

I have found that the majority of people in the West, whether or not they were delivered by one of these methods, flinch when they are mentioned. We have an innate knowing that something is amiss with these methods. Although they often save lives and are necessary in some cases, they are also often carried out when not necessary, which is one of the greatest tragedies of our Western birthing process. Sometimes the clinical way that they are carried out also adds to the birth trauma.

The instruments that are used in delivery can have a profound effect on the way we come into the world, and in this chapter we will explore their impact on our belief system and sense of self.

## C-section

Perhaps one of the most traumatic instrument deliveries is the C-section. It comes with a host of challenges that reverberate throughout life.

C-section people are often fearful that their rites of passage, for example, their first day of school or having their first period, have been unrecognised.

They can also be easily distracted or sidetracked from a set task and leave work unfinished. Sometimes their greatest desire is to find one task that completes them. They are either the people who never complete a task, or the ones that are up until 4 am, and will not go to bed until they've finished a task. This is because on a subconscious level, they are constantly trying to finish the task of being born.

C-section people also tend to panic over small disturbances and become frantic when things tend to get more complicated. They also have a tendency to crave affection, needing lots of loving and cuddles. They can end up being needy babies and children.[81]

In an interview I did with Rebecca Thompson of the Consciously Parenting Project, she described how being a C-section baby affects the way that she works.

"My mom had wanted a home birth but ended up in the hospital when she didn't progress. And so finally, at half past one in the morning, they decided to carry out a C-section," Rebecca told me.

Before our interview, she had spoken with Ray Castellino, (founder of BEBA – Building and Enhancing Bonding and Attachment), Rebecca said that she had asked, "So you know I was born by C-section. What does that say about me?"

He replied, "Because of the way that you come into the world, if it's a natural birth, there's a long progression, and the baby is actively involved. With a C-section, they are inside and then they are outside, so they have to become very quick processors."

"This is something that shows up in my life," Rebecca said, corroborating Castellino's assessment. "If you look at the body of my work, I am managing vast quantities of information and I can do it very quickly. I can do assessments with families very quickly. I can see the patterns that are going on very quickly."

Rebecca shared that this ability to process information very quickly is also apparent during transition times. "For me, I tend to transition very quickly. When I was told that I needed to go on a gluten-free diet, for example, I took in all the information at 2 in the afternoon, and by 4 in the afternoon, I was gluten-free."

The C-section was mirrored by multiple places in Rebecca's life. She revealed:

"One of the things that I know about myself is that when I am doing an interview, for example, I have to script out everything that I'm going to say at the beginning and end, with just a few bullet points in the middle. If I don't have something written down at the beginning and end, I fall apart. Ray Castellino highlighted that this mirrors my birthing experience. Before they carried out the C-section, the doctors knew exactly how it was going to start and end before they began. So that became part of my imprint too. It's fascinating when you start to look at it because it mirrors many different aspects of life."

Although there are some positive effects from the C-section, as Rebecca mentioned, it can also leave babies with a number of challenges. These include:

- Waking up at night
- Intensive crying
- Trauma crying
- Feeding difficulties
- Digestive difficulties (because they didn't go down the birth canal and pick up the gut flora that they needed)
- Colic (not being able to digest their food)
- Not wanting to be held
- Bonding difficulties[82]

---

### Julia and Radha – Elective C-section Birth Experience

Single mum Julia contacted me when her baby, Radha, was 11 weeks old. She was having problems breastfeeding Radha, who was very angry, resisting sleeping, and suffered with colic. Julia and Radha had been having homeopathic treatment for a number of weeks, which she found was helping, but there was clearly still something else that needed addressing.

---

Julia had previously broken her pelvis in a number of places and had torn her sciatic nerve during a horse riding accident. The hospital didn't pick up on these injuries and sent her home from hospital. Sixteen weeks later her injuries were picked up, by which time she had developed CRPS (complex regional pain syndrome).

There was still a lot of anger and sadness around this as she felt it had ended her life and she was angry with the doctors at the hospital because of how they reacted when they discovered their mistake.

When we discussed her pregnancy, she shared that Radha's conception was planned and she was wanted. However, Julia had felt regret, anger and worry about what effect her CRPS condition was having on her unborn baby during pregnancy. She had had to take very strong painkillers for two weeks when the pain became unbearable. She had also been worried about redundancy. In addition, her relationship with Radha's father was a complicated situation and a few of her friends and family were not supportive of her becoming pregnant and being a single parent.

Because of her injury, Julia had chosen to have a C-section because she felt her pelvis was not stable enough to go through the birthing process. However, the doctors said that they wanted her to try a natural birth. This caused Julia a lot of fear. In the end, the doctors agreed to the C-section and Julia was booked in for the operation one week before the hospital due date, which again caused her concern because she was worried Radha was going to come early.

During the C-section, the doctors had trouble administering the epidural into her spine because of the damage from the riding accident. It took over 45 minutes to administer the injection, which caused a lot of shock not only for Julia, but for her friend, who was her birthing partner. This was the only trauma during the birth as the rest of the

C-section went to plan and only took a few minutes to perform. Radha was put straight on Julia's chest and started breastfeeding within an hour.

However, during the night Radha cried solidly and the nurses took her away from Julia so she could sleep. Once home, Radha continued to cry unless Julia held her close on her chest. They later discovered she was tongue-tied (when an unusually short, thick membrane connects the underside of the tongue to the floor of the mouth), which hindered her breastfeeding, so at three weeks old they cut the tie. This helped a little. Radha was still angry before she went to sleep and she woke up angry too.

As we started the session Julia had a lot of grief and sadness, which was held in her womb. This went back to Julia's own birth experience, and we released it.

When we checked back there was still some grief remaining in her womb and we were taken to Radha's birth, relating to the C-section. The advice her younger self needed to hear was that "everything was going to be ok" and "this choice of having a C-section was not going to harm her baby".

We then moved to just after the C-section and found that Radha's ECHO was feeling furious because she was shouting her head off and nobody was taking any notice of her. She said she was "angry, cold and Mum's not there". The surgeons, who were there in the room, were all wearing masks, which frightened Radha. Radha was saying, "Who are these people and where's my mum? This isn't what I was expecting and I wasn't ready to come out!"

We found she had shock in her stomach, which we tapped on her and released. We reassured her she was safe. The energy in her stomach was soon released.

We checked the energy in Julia's womb and found that the grief had cleared and the picture she had was of Radha being held up by the surgeons laughing, instead of crying and being angry. We asked Radha if she was happy coming out that way and if she could choose differently, would she rather have come out the traditional way. Radha said she was happy and just wanted to be with Mum now, so we placed her on Julia's chest and held her close. She happily breastfed and bonded with Mum. In this picture, the sun is shining through the windows and everything is feeling and looking light. We checked Julia's body and it was strong and healthy. This is the picture we reimprinted.

A week after the session, I checked in with Julia to see how things were progressing and these are the results Julia gave me:
Radha being very angry was previously 10/10 and reduced to 3/10
Resisting sleep was previously 10/10 and reduced to 4/10
Colic – completely gone
Difficulty in sleeping at night-time was previously 10/10 and reduced to 0/10
Change in Julia's CRPS: chronic pain in the back and pelvis definitely better from 6/10 to 3/10 in the sacrum, 1/10 in pelvis.

When I asked Julia how she felt about her birth compared to before, she said, "When I call up memories I actually see a very peaceful birth, and even though I can rationalise that this is not the right memory, it *feels* right. I am accepting of when Radha gets angry and have stopped worrying about how it may affect her later in life."

C-sections can also create rescuer issues. If the baby receives the message that if they are in trouble somebody is going to rescue them, then they can go through life waiting or needing to be rescued, and even being attached to being rescued. On the other hand, they might have issues about being rescued, such as anger and resentment if they feel somebody is interfering in their life. This kind of conditioning can lead to inferiority complexes, including the belief that they weren't good enough to be able to do it on their own. There is also sometimes a guilt complex around the fact that their mother had to have surgery to give birth to them. C-section children can end up with poor self-esteem, and task difficulties (such as not being able to complete a task). And as mentioned above, they also might find themselves with boundary difficulties, including not being able to set boundaries or respect other people's boundaries, as their own personal boundaries were not respected by the surgeons.[83]

## Children Can Remember their Birth

Young children often remember their early experiences and will recount them to their parents when asked. They describe what it was like in the womb and how their birth experience was. Lesley shared with me her son's comments on remembering his birth. He clearly knew that he needed help to get out of the womb.

---

### Julian – Remembers his Birth

At Julian's birth, Lesley was in a lot of pain, especially in her back. She described her labour as back-breaking. The labour was not progressing so she was given an epidural, but unfortunately they gave her an overdose and it paralysed the whole of her body right up to her neck. She couldn't move her arms and was struggling to maintain her breathing, which was making her panic. Eventually, they ended up giving her a C-section. This is the story her son Julian shared with her as she was preparing for his third birthday party:

"Do you remember being born, Julian?" Lesley had asked him.
Julian went really quiet and replied, "Yes." He paused and then said, "I remember I tried to go in there and it was

---

too tight so I came back and I waited. Then I went and got a ladder, I climbed up to where the light was, and then your back wasn't broken any more." This was just as Lesley had described the pain in her back during the labour.

He then went on to say, "I remember I was so sad because you didn't pick me up." She explained to him that the doctors had given her too much medicine so she couldn't move. The medicine made her so scared and she wasn't able to hold him. "I'm sorry but I wasn't able to move," she said.

So he repeated that he had waited and gone and got the ladder to get out himself so it was OK. All the anger she had was healed at the point that he said he chose how to be born and he found his own way out. It was OK to have a C-section. We later did a Matrix Birth Reimprinting on the birth and gave her the experience of giving birth naturally.

## Deliveries by Forceps and Ventouse (Vacuum Extraction)

Forceps deliveries and ventouse deliveries have an effect similar to that of induction and augmentation, which we discussed in the previous chapter. We will concentrate mainly on forceps delivery throughout this section as a ventouse has the same effects as forceps.

With these kinds of deliveries the baby may end up with bonding difficulties, a loss of trust and, even when anaesthetics are used, a belief that human contact is painful. They can trigger:

- shock
- fear
- pain
- a sense of intrusion or violence
- coldness
- feeling invaded, violated and abused
- loss of control

They can also lead to a defensive reaction to being touched, cuddled or held.[84]

159

### 'Jeff' – Forceps Delivery
### by Ted Wilmont

I worked with a client, Jeff, who had myalgic encephalo-myelitis (ME/CFS or fibromyalgia). He was experiencing a significant amount of pressure in his head. Although this kind of pressure is common with this condition, I also had an intuition that something else might be causing this. I asked, "Did you have a forceps delivery?"

"How did you know that?" he replied.

Jeff had experienced a highly traumatic pre-birth. His mother was in an aircraft and they had to make a crash landing.

What was interesting about Jeff was that he had a big head for his body, and when he was born it was exceptionally red. He showed me a picture of himself as a child. He was wearing a red bobble hat. It was as though everything in Jeff's world was reinforcing the whole notion of having a red, swollen head.

We worked on the pre-birth trauma. For Jeff, there was a lot of red mist surrounding the crash landing. We worked on the forceps delivery, releasing the red from that too. It seemed the red was subconsciously linked with the inflammation he was experiencing, because as soon as we released the red, the pressure in his head began to change.

### 'Sarah and Simon' – Too Painful to be Touched

I worked with Sarah, the mother of a 14-year-old boy, Simon, who didn't want to be held or touched by his parents since birth. Although she wasn't aware of it at the time of his birth, his collarbone had been broken and this was added to the painful experience of the forceps delivery during the birthing process. Every time Sarah held him to feed him, baby Simon screamed, so she had to prop him up in a chair in order to bottle-feed him. It wasn't until three months later that the doctors finally discovered he had a broken collarbone. By that time, Simon had already made the decision that it was too painful to be touched and still objected to being held.

Using Matrix Birth Reimprinting, Sarah and I went back to the time of Simon's birth and she apologised to him for not realising he was in so much pain. We tapped on him for his pain and frustration at not being understood. We then guided him back through a healthy birth and bonding experience and reimprinted him happily breastfeeding.

The evening of the session he came into the kitchen with a friend whilst Sarah was washing up. He said, "Mum, I've hurt my back playing football, can you rub it for me?" After she had done so, he thanked her and gave her a huge hug. This was very atypical behaviour for him. In fact, this was the first time in his life that he had initiated contact with her.

Having a forceps delivery is extremely painful for the baby. It can also lead to children who are really angry, really withdrawn, anxious, depressed, and have ADD and ADHD.[85]

## Forceps Delivery and Feeling Stuck or Held Back in Life

As I highlighted previously, babies that have been born with a forceps delivery often feel pressured in life, and under someone else's authority. When they want to go for something, they actually feel stuck or held back.[86] Can you imagine starting a new career and wanting to put yourself out there, but ending up feeling stuck or held back, or even going into panic when you try? This is the experience of many adults who had forceps delivery as babies. In most cases, we don't correlate this fear with what happened at birth. There is also the added fear that something really pleasurable will turn into pain.[87]

In more extreme cases, the child or adult will repel touch, and may also have severe physical symptoms such as headaches. I've worked with a number of people who had headaches from forceps delivery. One client happened to mention to me that her son had severe headaches on a regular basis, and as soon as she mentioned a forceps delivery, I suspected that this might be responsible. She was an EFT and Matrix Reimprinting practitioner herself, and when he came home from school with a headache several days later, she carried out a Matrix Birth Reimprinting session with him and his headache went away and (as far as I am aware) did not return.

On another occasion, I was teaching Matrix Reimprinting and Matrix Birth Reimprinting in South Africa. Several days into the training, one of the men attending the course said, "You're going to have to excuse me today. I am here in person but if you happen to see me snoozing or just looking a bit vacant, it's not because I'm bored or tired, it's because I've had to take some really strong pain killers because I have one of my headaches."

I asked him about his birth. "Did you happen to have a forceps delivery?"

"Yes," he replied.

We carried out a Matrix Birth Reimprinting session. He had a great sense of humour, and when we worked on his ECHO in the womb, his baby self wanted to come out wearing an American footballer crash helmet, complete with visor. He also asked for something in his hand so that he wouldn't get stuck. We widened the passage and also gave him a magic wand, as per the request of his baby self.

I instructed him, "Come out in your own time," and he came out so quickly it was like he was on a slide at a water park! I said to him, "Would you like to go back and do it again?" because it was so much fun, and he said that he did. He was reborn several times, until he was ready to take off the helmet and relinquish the magic wand. His headaches went away for a month (which was unusual for him), but in this case, they did return. There may have been another aspect to this that we didn't uncover; however, I didn't get to work with him again and explore further.

It is important to note that not everything is resolved in a single session with this work, and sometimes deeper investigation is needed to explore aspects that may not have shown up in the first session.

## Craneo-osteopathy or Craniosacral Therapy – the Antidote to a Forceps Birth

I always recommend that parents take their child for a craneo-osteopathy or Craniosacral Therapy session if they have had a forceps delivery or vacuum extraction delivery. This needs to happen as soon as possible after birth. (In fact, it is generally recommended to have a craneo-osteopathy or Craniosacral Therapy session after birth, regardless of what the birth was like.)

In a session, a practitioner will work with the fluid that circulates around the brain and down through the spine. They also help the bones of the skull to realign and go back into place. This is because, for six weeks after birth, the skull bones are movable plates connected by connective tissue, which later become fixed. The bones in the skull need to be more flexible and can move over each other so the baby's head can navigate through the birth canal more easily. That's why it is advisable to carry out the treatment as soon as possible. You'll know babies that have been born by forceps or vacuum extraction because their heads look Martian-like. Their head has been extended up, and although it does go back into a relatively normal shape, the bones need help to settle back into where they should be. I've witnessed amazing things that happen for babies after a craneo-osteopathy or Craniosacral Therapy session. Babies who were having trouble breastfeeding start feeding normally. Their sleep patterns improve, their tendency to have colic reduces and they generally are happier and more settled. Other benefits include reduction in allergies and ear infection.[88]

Throughout Part 3, we have focused on some of the more common birth traumas that occur in the West. Later, in Chapter 15, we will explore some of the more specific experiences that are not common to most individuals, and can create birth trauma for those involved.

Now that we have covered some of the more common birth challenges that can create separation and isolation for the baby, in Part 4 we will learn how to rewrite these traumas with Matrix Birth Reimprinting.

# Part 4

# Matrix Birth Reimprinting

# Chapter 12

# Matrix Birth Reimprinting

*Whenever and however you give birth, your experience will impact your emotions, your mind, your body, and your spirit for the rest of your life.*
**Ina May Gaskin**

We have looked at some of the common birth traumas that occur in the Western birthing process. We have also explored how the consciousness of the baby is something that has been misunderstood, and that when we perceive the baby as a conscious being, we start to realise the damage that may have occurred and which may have reverberated throughout the rest of its life.

So far, much of this book has focused on the problem of the way that we birth our children in the Western world. The technique that follows offers a solution to rewrite any birth trauma that may have occurred. It includes traumas that occurred from conception, while in utero, and at birth itself.

There are many similarities to the conventional Matrix Reimprinting technique in the Matrix Birth Reimprinting work. But there are also some vital differences. We will explore these throughout the following chapter.

You will also notice that this protocol addresses many of the issues we have highlighted in this book, such as initiating the bonding process and healing any issues that may have occurred around separation. As you are already familiar with the EFT and Matrix Reimprinting tapping techniques (see Part 1), in this chapter we will go straight into the Matrix

Birth Reimprinting protocol, so that you can experience it.

It is important to note that I usually recommend that someone be present with you to reimprint your birth. You can do these techniques on yourself, but the effects are far more powerful if someone such as an experienced Matrix Birth Reimprinting practitioner guides you through the protocol.

Whilst I address Matrix Reimprinting practitioners in the next two chapters, I encourage non-practitioners to read them too.

## Matrix Birth Reimprinting Process
### Coming into the World

The process starts at the time when the baby is about to be born. If there are issues in the womb leading up to the birth, then it is important to clear these first. You can shrink yourself down inside the womb and tap on the foetus at any point during the conception or pregnancy, just as you would tap on any ECHO in Matrix Reimprinting. I want to make it clear at this stage that, just like in Matrix Reimprinting, it is crucial to clear the trauma before you reimprint the birth. It isn't simply about creating a new picture over an old one and replacing the memory. It is about clearing the trauma and then putting a new picture in its place. If you are new to these tools, I recommend reviewing the chapters on EFT and Matrix Reimprinting. For further study, see *Matrix Reimprinting Using EFT* by Karl Dawson and Sasha Allenby, and *Transform Your Beliefs, Transform Your Life* by Karl Dawson and Kate Marrilat. Details of trainings to become a qualified EFT, Matrix Reimprinting, and Matrix Birth Reimprinting practitioner can be found at the back of this book under "Matrix Reimprinting and EFT Resources".

Assuming you are working with an ECHO that is about to be born, one of the first things you might find is that they aren't ready to come into the world. This is often tied up with the belief that the world is a dangerous place. It may be a belief from a previous lifetime. You can clear this using the Matrix Birth Reimprinting protocol, tapping to release the fear from the unborn baby's body and reassuring them that it is safe. This will usually switch the belief to 'The baby really wants to be born now,' or even, 'The baby's excited about being born.' We want your client's ECHO to be ready for birth before we proceed.

### Setting up the delivery space
Once your client's ECHO is ready to be born, set up their delivery space.

### Where
The first consideration is where the baby would like to be born. They may choose a hospital or a home birth. Quite often they want to be born somewhere in nature with any combination of water, earth, trees, flowers, birds and animals. I've also had numerous babies wanting to be born in a tepee or a pyramid. Sometimes people want to be born in a different part of the world to where they were actually born. Anywhere is fine, as long as your client's ECHO has chosen this.

### Who
The next consideration is who is going to be present at the birth and who is going to be there to assist the mother. The baby can also choose who is going to receive them into the world. The father is the usual choice for receiving the baby but it could also be the mother herself, the midwife, angels (who are often there at birth), or the client's older self. You can ask the baby who they would like and trust to receive them. Once you've set the scene, double-check that the baby is ready to be born. Ensure that the excitement is still there.

Quite often I will ask the client, "What's the connection like between your mother and your baby self (the ECHO)?" You are looking for a strong, loving and healthy connection and for there to be love between them. If love and trust is not present, work with them until it is. You can ask questions, such as "How does your baby self feel in there? Is there a strong connection with Mum? Is your baby self (the ECHO) still ready to be born? How safe is she/he feeling? How excited are they about coming into the world? Is there anything else that is needed?"

## Association

Once there is love, trust, and excitement about entering the world, ask your client to imagine becoming the baby. This is called association, and it is where Matrix Birth Reimprinting differs from Matrix Reimprinting. In the Matrix Reimprinting protocol, the recipient always remains separate from the ECHO. With Matrix Birth Reimprinting it is different. This is because your client, as the recipient, needs to go through the process physically for the new birth.

In the book *Matrix Reimprinting Using EFT*, authors Karl Dawson and Sasha Allenby shed light on why this is the case. When I first started doing this technique, I shared with Karl and Sasha that in Matrix Birth Reimprinting, the client had to associate with the baby in order for it to be reborn. Their initial reaction was a definite No, because the whole premise of Matrix Reimprinting is dissociation so that the client doesn't get re-traumatised by the experience. However, Sasha decided to experiment. She spent several months using the Matrix Birth Reimprinting protocol on volunteers. She used the protocol with 50% of them dissociated and 50% of them associated. At the end of the experiment, she came back to me and said, "You're right. People really need to be associated to get those physical changes activated. It became really apparent right at the start of the experiment." Once he had thought through the process, Karl agreed.

The key is, you would not want your client to associate with the baby when they are traumatised. But it is a totally different matter associating with them when they are experiencing positive emotions. It is the positive energy that the client is connecting with. It is similar to when you are doing the Matrix Reimprinting technique. At the end of the technique, the reimprinting process is associated – you take the positive picture into your body in order to be able to experience it. Similarly, your client goes through the birth in order to feel it.

Once your client is associated, double check to make sure they are still ready to be born. Sometimes when the client associates, new things can come up that the baby self (ECHO) may not have told your client. As the practitioner, make sure to remember to change your language here from asking "How is your ECHO feeling?" to "How are you feeling in the womb?"

Other suggestions are:
- What does it feel like in there?
- What does that connection with Mum feel like?
- Are you still ready to be born?
- Is there anything else that is needed before you are born?

### Starting the Birth Process

Again, check that there is an association with the ECHO. You will often notice a visual change when there is. Sometimes, but not always, the recipient will appear to be in a deep trance state. You can say something along the lines of:

"You are going to feel gentle waves of energy sending you down towards the light. And just know that your father (or whoever they have chosen to receive them after they have been born) is going to be on the other side. I'm going to give you space to go through this process on your own. Take your time, come out in your own time, this is your birth process. Just let me know when you're out."

Then hold the space for them and sit silently during the process. There is no need to tap as it can be off-putting for the client. If they are there with you in person, you can just hold their hand.

As soon as they have been born, you will likely see physical signs in the recipient. Their face and their body movement will change. One client, who took over fifteen minutes to be born, shuddered when she came out of the womb. I asked her if she was OK and she replied, "Oh yes, that was just my legs coming out."

### Once the Baby is Out

Once they have been through the birth canal, ask whoever received them to place them on the mother's abdomen so they can crawl up to her arms, or alternatively place them in their mother's arms. In the early days of this protocol, I always instructed people to place the baby on the mother's abdomen so that it could crawl to her chest (we discussed

171

the reasons behind this in Chapter 10). However, later on in the process I started to realise that it was just as effective to place them in the mother's arms. Which is appropriate is a matter of intuition in each case session.

### Bonding with the Mother
Once the baby is lying in its mother's arms, instruct them to connect with her through their six senses (sight, hearing, smell, taste, body feeling, emotional feeling).

1  Sight: Making eye-to-eye contact: "Look deep into your mother's eyes and allow her to look deep into yours."

2  Hearing: Ask them, "What you can hear?" It could be the sound of their mother's or father's voice, it could be the mother's heartbeat. If they want to share what they can hear then that is fine, but there is no pressure for them to do so. Sometimes just asking the question is enough to initiate the sense.

3  Smell: Ask, "What can you smell?" It may be the smell of their mother, or her milk or her perfume. It is sometimes the smell of flowers, or the smell of talcum powder.

4  Taste: Ask, "What can you taste?" It may be the taste of the milk, or the mother's skin.

5  Touch: Ask, "How does the skin contact feel?" "How does your body feel being held?"

6  Our sixth sense is our empathic, intuitional and emotional feeling state. Ask them, "How does it feel emotionally being held in your mother's arms?" or "Are you experiencing any emotions right now?" They may reply that they feel safe, peaceful, loving, connected, or trusting. Ask them to distinguish the difference between their emotions and the emotions of their mother and father by asking how their parents feel.

Sometimes they want to go through the bonding process with their father too, so give them that option and repeat the eye-to-eye contact with their dad.

### Reimprinting the Picture

Before you reimprint the picture, check that it is complete by asking them if there is anything else they need. For example, they may need a new resource, someone else to enter the room, or anything else that would make the picture even more positive.

In the next part of the protocol, they go back to being dissociated. So, when it feels as though the picture is complete, ask them to step out of their baby self and look at the picture from the outside. Check what emotions they feel when looking at the picture. You are looking for a response of peace, love, connection, joy, safety, and so on.

Ask them what colour is in and around the picture. Then instruct them to take the picture in through the top of their head, allowing the mind to reconnect to the new colours and emotions.

Next, ask them take the picture into their heart and send the coloured energy around the body to every cell. Make the picture bigger and brighter and then use the heart to send the picture out into the universe. (See Chapter 7 for a reminder of the importance of the heart and its field in this work.) Remind them to connect with the colour that was surrounding the image.

The most frequently chosen colours for Matrix Birth Reimprinting are:
- Pink (heals separation, represents unconditional love and balances the feminine energies)
- Blue (promotes trust and faith and gives us back our voice. Also balances the masculine energies)
- Gold (empowerment, wisdom and knowledge)
- Rainbow (rainbow colours make up white light and bring balance to everything)

Instruct them to finish by reconnecting to their baby self in their heart and by asking their baby self if they have anything else they would like to share with them before finishing.

**Summary of the Matrix Birth Reimprinting Protocol from a Practitioner's Point of View**

1  Check that the baby is ready to come into the world. Clear any issues or traumas that are preventing them from wanting to enter the world.

2  Set up the delivery space – who is going to receive them? Where do they want to be born? What is the environment of the space like? What specific colours are present?

3  Once the baby is ready to be born, instruct the recipient to associate with their baby self (become them).

4  Allow the gentle waves of energy to take the recipient (as their baby self), down the birth canal.

5  Once the baby is out, place them on the mother's abdomen or breast.

6  Bonding – allow bonding to take place through all the senses. Remember, the eye-to-eye contact is vital for stimulating the cingulate gyrus.

7  Reimprint the picture. Instruct your recipient to dissociate from the picture so they are looking at it from the outside. Instruct them to take the picture and everything associated with this picture in through the top of their head, through the cells in their body and then into their heart. Make the colours brighter in the heart and use the heart to send the energy around the body to every cell, and then transmit the picture out into the universe.

Now that you have the basics of the Matrix Birth Reimprinting protocol, in the next chapter we will explore how to find memories in the womb when they are buried in the subconscious.

# Chapter 13

## Working with Your Baby Self In the Womb

*As I unclutter my life, I free myself to answer the callings of my soul.*
**Dr Wayne Dyer**

The one question I get asked most frequently in my work with Matrix Birth Reimprinting is how to find subconscious or blocked memories. In this chapter I will share a number of different tools that will enable you to connect with your baby self in the womb, even if you have no conscious memories of being there. Some of these tools are classic Matrix Reimprinting techniques, and some I have adapted for Matrix Birth Reimprinting.

In the latter part of this chapter, after you have found the baby self in the womb, we will explore in more detail how to work with the baby self, or ECHO, to change beliefs and release trauma.

### How to Find a Memory in the Womb
There are six methods for finding a memory in the womb.

### Method One – Follow the Energy
The most popular way of finding a subconscious memory comes from a classic Matrix Reimprinting technique. It involves tuning in to where the energy is in the body and following that feeling back to the memory. For example, if you have a sadness or heaviness in your heart when you think about your birth, drop into this sadness and focus on it as you start to tap. On many occasions this has taken clients back to a 'memory' of

being in the womb where the sadness was created.

The tapping often helps us to tune into subconscious/unconscious memories that are not present for us when we try to think of them with the conscious mind.

I often describe this process by using a computer as a metaphor. Imagine that an individual memory is like a Word document or an Excel spreadsheet that you would like to open and read. First you need to focus on opening the programme, which you would normally do by clicking on the icon on your desktop. Sometimes we take a short cut and use the file manager or have the file itself on our desktop for easy access; other times we need to run a search to find what we are looking for. Once you have found and opened the programme, you then click on the next icon or folder that represents the document you want to open. The document opens and there are all the details you need contained within the document. Now imagine your body is your computer desktop. By putting your attention on, and tuning into, the feeling within your body, you are helping to identify, first the programme, and then the file you would like to open to access the information contained in that memory. And if you do not consciously know where to find it, tapping on the body feeling helps to tune you in, like running a search in your file manager. If this method does not work for you, there are five other methods that help you access a subconscious memory.

### Method Two – Going Back Down the Timeline

Another method is to identify the feeling in the body and then, as you tap, picture yourself going back down your timeline, i.e. backwards through your life, to where the memory was created.

If you are doing these techniques on your own or with a client, it can be helpful to use an approach similar to that of Time Line Therapy – a tool from Neuro-Linguistic Programming. Tune into the feeling in the body and then float above the body so you are looking at the timeline of your life from above. Go back down the timeline, seeing yourself getting younger and younger and younger until a memory

176

connected to the theme emerges. This technique can also be used to uncover past life memories.

Whether you are doing this work as a therapist or on yourself, it is important to return to the present moment. For example, when you initially float above the timeline, place a flag marked '*now*' at the present moment. This enables you to locate and return to the present moment.

If you are a practitioner using these tools on clients, you can also ask questions that lead them back down the timeline. Ask them to take you back according to age. Have them tune into the feeling and then ask, "Was that feeling there when you were 20 years old?" If the feeling is still the same in the body, continue on with, "How about when you were 15? How about when you were 10? Was it there when you were 5?" And so on.

When you get to a certain age, sometimes the client will say something like, "I've still got that feeling in my throat or chest, but it's changed a bit." If this occurs, it is best to make a note of it for a later session because there might be an ECHO to go back to who is running a similar theme to what was set up in the womb.

When you get closer to birth you can ask, "Was that feeling there after birth? How about before birth? Was it there in the third trimester/ the second/the first? How about at conception?"

Wherever the feeling dissipates, you know that you are roughly in the right area. Ask them to imagine seeing themselves at whatever age you got to before the feeling disappeared. For example, if it was in the third trimester in the womb, instruct them to see the baby in the womb. You can then ask them to shrink themselves down into the womb and tap on their baby self for the issue you are working with.

**Method Three – Working ECHO to ECHO**

In Matrix Reimprinting there is something called an 'ECHO string'. This is where a number of ECHOs exist on the same life theme. In other words, due to an early traumatic event, we attract or create a number of similar experiences on the same theme until the issue is resolved. ECHO strings are a very helpful way of getting us and our clients back to subconscious memories. For example, say you are working on an ECHO for which you have a memory on a particular theme. While you are with that ECHO, you can ask them to take you back to an earlier memory on the same theme. What happens in the large majority of cases is that the ECHO takes you back to an earlier memory. Sometimes it is something that you are already aware of in your conscious mind. Other times it is something that you weren't aware of or had forgotten about.

**Method Four – Matrix Recall Technique**
Another method to help you (or a client) recall a subconscious memory is the Matrix Recall technique (also known as "Slow EFT").

Say, for example, you have some anger in the chest and you don't know where it's coming from. You can start tapping slowly on one single point with your eyes closed. Starting on the top of your head and remaining there for some time, repeat the reminder phrase, 'All this anger in my chest,' every now and again. It is important to carry out this technique slowly and hypnotically. Leaving gaps between repeating the reminder phrase will create space for a memory on a particular theme or topic to emerge. If no memory emerges, move onto the next point and continue tapping slowly until a memory does come up.

**Method Five – Before, During or After?**
Another method is to tune into the current feeling, tap, and ask the client (or yourself), "Did this happen before, during or after birth?" Take the first answer. If the client answers, "I'm not sure," it is likely that they are in their thinking mind. If this is the case, instruct them to draw attention to their heart or to go to the place from where they receive inner guidance in order to give you an answer.

**Method Six – Imagining Yourself in the Womb**
Sometimes uncovering a subconscious memory in Matrix Birth Reimprinting is as simple as asking your client (or yourself) if they can see themselves in the womb. If your client is not visual, you can also ask them to sense or imagine themselves there. It is worth noting that sometimes

a client can get blocked when they are asked to see, or visualize something, because they expect a TV screen to open up in their mind, but it is often much more subtle than that.

You can teach people to visualize. Ask your client to imagine their front door, or describe their mother or child, for example. The type of picture that springs to mind on an occasion like this often opens a door to visualizing the ECHO or memory.

## How to Work with the Baby Self in the Womb

Once you've found the baby self or ECHO, whether it is in the womb or at the time of birth, you can work with them in the same way that you would with an ECHO in Matrix Reimprinting.

Step into the picture and tap on them, asking what emotion they are feeling. Find out what the emotion is and where it is located in the body, and then tap on the ECHO for the emotion.

For example:

Tapping on the Karate Chop Point: Even though you have got all this anger in your chest, you're still a beautiful baby.

Top of the Head: All this anger.

Eyebrow: This anger in your chest.

Side of the Eye: All this anger.

Under the Eye: It's safe to release some of this now.

(And so on, throughout all the points, and continuing until the emotion is released.)

## Who Does It Belong To?

When I am working with a client, we ask their ECHO in the womb who the emotion belongs to. Often the emotion initially feels like it belongs to the ECHO, but we discover that they have actually picked it up from their mother, their father, or someone else.

When you ask the question "Who does it belong to?", the recipient starts to see how they had perceived the energy as their own when it actually belonged to someone else.

You can ask your client what percentage belongs to their ECHO and what percentage belongs to somebody else. Often they will say something like 80% belongs to somebody else and 20% belongs to the ECHO. If it belongs purely to the ECHO, then you work exclusively with them. When the larger percentage comes from the parents or someone else, you can imagine tapping on them whilst at the same time helping the ECHO to realise that it doesn't belong to them.

You can ask the ECHO if it is OK to let go of the emotion that doesn't belong to them. Most people will say yes, but sometimes you will come across some resistance. In these cases, there is usually a belief that they need to hold onto the emotion as it is helping Mum or Dad, or there is a fear of letting it go. (Thinking of your current life right now, if your mother, father or partner is angry or fearful and you are feeling empathy with that emotion, does your family member feel less anger or fear because you are also feeling it? The answer is of course No, but we often have the belief that by holding this emotion we are helping them to feel better. Alternatively, it could be that we feel it is helping us to be more connected to our parent, or it's our responsibility to hold on to this emotion.)

By explaining to the ECHO that they are not helping Mum or Dad by holding this energy, they will be able to release it through tapping, or it will fade once they have had the realisation that it is not theirs. You can also bring a colour frequency into the emotional block to change (or release) it.

Whoever has the biggest share of the emotion is the one you tap on first. If it is the mother, you can let the ECHO of the baby know that you are going to leave the womb and tap directly on the ECHO of the mother. When you work on the parent, you are resourcing them with what they need to feel safe and supported in the given situation.

## Dissociation and Association

If there is a positive event or positive feeling that comes up whilst working with the ECHO in the womb, it is vital to associate in that moment. Association is where the recipient lives or relives the event as if it were happening now. The key thing to understand about association is that the subconscious mind does not recognise any time frame, so if your client associates with a positive feeling or emotion, the subconscious experiences it as though it is happening now.

One example of where you may instruct someone to associate is when you are taking a mother back through giving birth to her child and rewriting it as a positive experience. Although she may not have experienced it as pleasurable the first time, birth can be an ecstatic experience. If you watch the film *Organic Birth* (formerly known as *Orgasmic Birth*), you will see that many women experience orgasms during labour.

The trailer of *Organic Birth* can be found on the membership site. Please see details at the end of this book.

However, we have been entrained to believe that childbirth can only be painful. This collective belief means that we automatically associate childbirth with pain, and continually reinforce it to be so.

Another time you will associate is if you are re-experiencing your own birth (or you are taking your client through a Reimprinting of their own birth).

Just to be clear, you may experience association and dissociation simultaneously. Sometimes you experience being reborn and witnessing your own birth at the same time.

So when you are inside the womb, feel what it felt like to be in the womb. This includes evoking the associated positive emotions.

The key time to dissociate is when the ECHO is experiencing negative emotion. If you (or your client) associate with the ECHO when they are distressed, the negative emotion will be experienced and this is not necessary. In Chapter 4 we discussed how the key difference between EFT and Matrix Reimprinting is that in EFT we take the negative emotion back into the body in order to resolve it, whereas in Matrix Reimprinting, we can resolve it without re-experiencing it. Dissociation means you can work with the emotion without re-experiencing it. It causes less stress to the body and the recipient.

Sometimes you may get your client to associate and then something negative happens with the baby, i.e. they get caught in the birth canal or the cord gets wrapped around their neck. It might be that these things happened in the original birth but the client didn't 'remember' until they were reimprinting the birth. If this occurs, get them to dissociate immediately, tap to resolve the issue and release whatever the baby was holding onto emotionally. Then re-associate your client and go back and start the birthing process again. You can do this as many times as you need to until the associated experience is a totally pleasant one from start to finish.

We associate when the ECHO is feeling positive emotion because association with them will ensure you are able to fully experience this too. Positive emotion triggers the chemicals associated with peace, love, joy and bliss in your body. Naturally, you benefit from these positive emotions circulating throughout your system. (When you are experiencing these emotions, your DHEA levels rise and your cortisol levels fall.)

Now that we have explored how to find ECHOs and work with them in the womb, in the next chapter we will take a deeper look at rewriting beliefs as part of the Matrix Birth Reimprinting Process.

# Chapter 14

# Rewriting Beliefs

*I need one of those baby monitors from my subconscious to my consciousness so I can know what the hell I'm really thinking about.*
**Steven Wright**

Our beliefs shape the way we filter the world and the way we see reality.

In Chapter 4, we explored one of the fundamental concepts in the conventional Matrix Reimprinting process, and how rewriting beliefs can have a profound impact on our health and wellbeing, as well as how we see the world.

In my work with Matrix Birth Reimprinting, I came to understand that many beliefs are shaped in the womb and at birth, as well as at conception.

In the womb, as we pointed out earlier, these beliefs are often shaped because the baby self does not know the difference between itself and its mother. Babies do not have the capacity to recognise that if their mother is shocked because she is pregnant, for example, this doesn't mean there is something wrong with them. They often take on the energy of what is happening in the womb as if it were their own, and shape a lifetime of significance based on the emotions that they felt.

As babies we have no reference point for who we were before these emotions were triggered, so we come into the world identified with them. We think they are us. And we subsequently shape a belief system based upon them.

One of the key factors here is that the beliefs and the emotions

183

become entangled. They feel real. And we respond accordingly. So, much of the work with Matrix Birth Reimprinting is to enable us to know ourselves beyond the beliefs and emotions that we have been conditioned with. It helps us to create new and supportive beliefs which help us thrive, as opposed to limiting beliefs which cause us to live from our smallness. When we live from our smallness, we are filtering the world through the eyes of the ECHO, rather than experiencing it through the present moment. So, in many ways, this work helps us to experience life beyond the filters and programmes that our beliefs create.

In this chapter, we will explore how beliefs are created, how they can be rewritten, and also how ECHOs are created for the baby in a traumatic event.

## The Power of Perception

In her book $E^2$, Pam Grout, well-known author of Law of Attraction books, shows how her father's flippant comment when she was born set up a pattern of insecurity throughout her whole adult life.

> When I was born on February 17, 1956, my father took one look at me, lying there helplessly in my pink bassinet, and announced to my mother that I was the ugliest baby he had ever seen. Needless to say, my mother was devastated. And for me, a minute-old human being, it was decided that beauty – or lack thereof – was destined to colour every moment of my life.
>
> My dad's life-changing indictment was prompted by my nose, which was plastered to my face like a roadkill possum. After my mother was in labour for 18 gruelling hours, her obstetrician decided to intervene with a pair of cold metal forceps. In the battle between forceps and me, my nose got flattened.
>
> Gradually, the nose bounced back to normal, but my fragile ego remained disfigured. I desperately wanted to be beautiful. I wanted to prove to my father that I was acceptable and to make up to my mother for the embarrassment I caused her.
>
> I scoured beauty magazines, studying the models like a biologist

studies cells. I rolled my hair with orange juice cans and ordered green facemasks and blackhead pumps from the back of Seventeen magazine. I saved my allowance to buy a set of Clairol rollers. I wore gloves to bed to keep the hand-softening Vaseline from staining the sheets. I even clipped 'interesting' hairstyles from the Montgomery Ward catalogue, pasting them to the back page of my own personal 'beauty book'.

This personal beauty book, besides the 50 heads with different hairstyles, listed my beauty goals: reduce my waist by five inches, increase my bust size by six inches, grow my hair, and so on. I even included a page with plans for accomplishing each goal. To reduce my waist for example, I would do 50 sit-ups each day, limit my morning pancake consumption to two, and give up Milky Way bars.

Despite my well-meaning attempts, I remained less than beautiful. No matter what I did, I never could seem to get my looks together. How could I? My very existence centred around my dad's ugly-baby statement. It was the first sentence about my life, the proclamation around which my very life revolved. To go against it would dishonour everything I knew – my dad, my mom, myself.

Things went from bad to worse. By sixth grade, my eyesight weakened and I was forced to wear a pair of horn-rimmed glasses. By ninth grade, when I finally convinced Dad to invest in contact lenses, a definite beauty booster, my face immediately broke out in a connect-the-dots puzzle of pimples. All my babysitting money went for Clearasil, astringent, and Angel Face Makeup. One summer, after I heard zits were caused by chocolates and soft drinks, I even gave up Coca-Cola and candy bars.

And if that wasn't bad enough, my sister, who had the good fortune to escape the forceps and the ugliness indictment, pointed out that my front teeth were crooked. Once again, I campaigned for family funds to install braces.

The sad thing about all this work and effort is that it was futile. I had no idea that until I changed the deep-seated thoughts about myself, I'd remain "ugly". I could have exercised, applied makeup, and rolled my hair unto eternity, but as long as my dad's indictment was the thought virus on which I operated, I was destined to be the "ugliest baby" he'd ever seen. Oh sure, I made temporary progress. I'd clear up my complexion or grow my hair or straighten my teeth, but before long, something else would happen to resume the old familiar "ugliness."

You see, my body had no choice but to follow the blueprints my thoughts had given it.

About this time, I discovered self-help books. It was an inevitable meeting. Any college freshman who thinks she closely resembles Frankenstein needs all the self-esteem boosting she can find.

I started with *Your Erroneous Zones*, by Dr Wayne Dyer, I read Barbara Walters' book on how to make conversation. I learnt how to win friends and influence people, how to empower myself with positive thinking, and how to think and grow rich. All the reading eventually started to change the way I felt about myself. I actually started finding things I liked.

Even things about my looks. I was tall, for one thing, which meant I could more or less eat anything I wanted and not gain weight. And my thick hair was an asset. And my best friend's mother said I had perfectly shaped eyebrows. Instead of looking at things I disliked, I started concentrating on things I liked. Like magic, my looks started to improve. As I gave up the limiting thoughts, I began to see my own beauty. The less I chastised that poor little ogre in the mirror, the more she started to change. The less I tried to change myself, the more I changed.

Miraculously, my eyesight returned to normal. I was finally able to throw away the Coke-bottle glasses and the contacts. The complexion from hell cleared up, and my teeth, after months of using a retainer, began to match the even teeth of the other members of the family. In fact, the only time I felt grotesquely ugly was when I'd visit my dad and his second wife.

Although I didn't realise it at the time, I was changing my "looks" during those visits to satisfy my dad's belief about me – or rather what

186

I thought were his beliefs about me. I now know my dad's remark was simply an offhand comment. He meant no harm.

But because I didn't know it at the time, I took his ugly-baby comment to heart and acted it out in rich, vivid detail. Even the poor eyesight, which some might argue is a genetic propensity, was solely my creation. Nobody else in my family (there are five of us) ever wore glasses. Everyone else had 20/20 vision. Likewise, nobody else in my family wore braces. They all had picture-perfect teeth.[89]

As you can see from Pam's experience, what we hear at birth really matters. The following session highlights how beliefs can be created by our Western birthing methods. In this case, the use of drugs to speed up the procedure helped create them.

---

### Discovering the Origin of the Core Belief: 'I'm not good enough'
### By Crystal Di Domizio – Prenatal Coach

The belief that I am not good enough is one that I struggled with for years. I felt like it was showing up both directly and indirectly in every area of my life.

I went into a Matrix Reimprinting session with the intention of getting to the root of this limiting belief. During the process I had a strong intuition that it started in the womb. Going back into the womb, I discovered that while my mom was giving birth, something occurred that had made me internalize the belief that I was not good enough.

As I was in the process of being born, a doctor told my mother that I was coming out too slowly so he administered her with synthetic oxytocin to speed up the labour.

I internalized what had happened into the belief that I was not good enough because I had been given the message that I was not entering the world effectively in the way that was expected. This had reverberations down my whole life.

---

> Through the Matrix Birth Reimprinting process, I allowed my mother's birth to unfold naturally, without any interference. I was able to take my time being born, and the birth was gentle and peaceful for my mother too. My colleague Kathleen helped me facilitate this session and I was amazed at the shifts I felt in me following that. The belief no longer had the same kind of resonance after the session.

## Survival Imprints

Birth Trauma expert Karen Melton coined the phrase 'survival imprints', and it is one that I have come to use frequently. Any situation where our life is under threat, or where we are in fight or flight and our system becomes over stimulated, can create an ECHO or a survival imprint. ECHOs and survival imprints are essentially the same thing. "ECHO" is the specific terminology used in Matrix Reimprinting, but in other systems of reference they are often called survival imprints. Any fear, terror or anxiety can cause a survival imprint. They are put into place to warn us that something in our external environment might be a threat to our survival. They are a subconscious learning. Survival imprints ultimately create beliefs, because what we learn in that moment we save later for our own protection.

Allergies can come from a survival imprint. If something traumatic happens when we are, say, eating an orange, the subconscious may store the information that oranges are not safe, as it mixes the external trigger with what we are ingesting. I also find that a lot of allergies go back to the womb or birth. Allergies can be triggered by the belief that the world is a dangerous place, as our body assesses harmless things in our environment as being unsafe. We can also inherit allergies from our mother, although there is no biological reason why this would be the case. We pick them up energetically. If you have inherited an allergy you can ask, "Who does this belong to?" and if it is not yours, you can return it to the earth or return it to where it originally came from with consciousness and love. (This is not a Matrix Birth Reimprinting protocol, but rather a tool that we are borrowing from another system, called Access Consciousness, created by Gary Douglas.)

As mentioned in Chapter 2, I have yet to work with somebody who was an IVF baby – I have only worked with mothers of IVF children and have assisted mothers (in sessions) through the IVF process. However, it would seem to me that this is a time when an ECHO or survival imprint can be created. In the early years of IVF, an over-abundance of viable eggs would be placed in the mothers' wombs, because doctors were unsure how many would implant. If too many eggs implanted, the doctors would abort some of them. From my point of view, the eggs that weren't aborted would most likely be aware of the loss of their siblings. And from a soul-consciousness point of view, these aware eggs were first surrounded by many other souls, and then many of them were killed. This must surely have created survival imprints. Nowadays, only one or two viable eggs are implanted at a time, avoiding this. It would be very interesting to explore what beliefs, if any, are created for those babies conceived in a test tube and also for those frozen as an egg.

Surgery in the womb can create an ECHO. If the baby has a cleft palate, doctors will operate on it in the womb because it is easier to fix in utero than it is after the baby is born. Surgery such as this can create an ECHO, especially if the foetus is conscious at the time. And, as previously discussed, if the mother is anaesthetised this would also have an effect on the baby. (See Chapter 10 for the effects of anaesthetics on the baby.)

Violence in the family can also cause an ECHO, especially if the mother either witnesses it or experiences it. Also, women who beat their husbands up (this is more common than many people like to think) and have a lot of anger and rage could cause an ECHO, as the baby will be experiencing the emotions of the mother.

Equally, when babies are unwanted, this can create an ECHO, particularly if the mother is considering an abortion or the abortion fails. Normally this occurs in the earlier stages of pregnancy when the mother discovers that she is pregnant and debates whether she is going to keep the child. If this describes you and you are in your first trimester of pregnancy, put your hand on your womb and tell your baby that you are sorry, that you were shocked, that you are happy they are here, and that they are safe.

When one child has been lost from the womb, whether it was through a miscarriage, stillbirth or abortion, this can leave an energy imprint in the womb, which the following child can empathically pick up on, and an ECHO can be created.

A survival imprint or ECHO can also be created if there is any life threat to the mother, i.e. if she is part of, or if she witnessed, a traumatic or shocking event, as the baby can process their mother's shock as their own.

Unstable mothers can also create a survival imprint in the unborn child. If the mother suffers from bipolar disorder, or any similar mental illness, then the uncertainty of the highs and lows can imprint on the child.

Sometimes a survival imprint is created by the fertilization process itself. Before the baby is conceived, the egg comes down the fallopian tube, is fertilized by the sperm, and then has to find somewhere to implant. Often when I speak about this on training courses, a number of people get triggered by the fear of not being able to find a safe place to be. This often manifests in a need to move from home to home in later life, trying to find a place that feels right.

I once worked with a client who went back to just before conception and was able to pick up on the energy from his father's sperm. He didn't know his father, but he sensed that there was some form of PTSD being conveyed through the sperm. When we cleared this, his general anxiety in life reduced significantly.

If fear has been triggered within you while reading any of the survival imprint descriptions, you may like to complete the following exercise to help you identify where the fear has come from.

### Writing Down Your Fears
This is a process I discovered before I started writing this book. In fact, this book probably would not have been written if I hadn't performed the exercise in Lawrence Block's book *Write for Your Life*[90] and taken the time to do this exercise. I have adapted this exercise from the book and combined it with EFT.

We often don't name the thing we fear. We believe if we put our attention on the fear, then we will make it worse or reinforce it. In fact, the opposite is true. We cannot change anything until we become conscious of it and stop sweeping it under the mat. Writing is a great way to access our subconscious, and a great way to find our limiting beliefs.

This exercise works for any subject you choose to use it with. Here, we will focus on "the fear of being born" or if you are a parent-to-be, then you can use "the fear of giving birth" or "the fear of being a parent", for example.

The first thing to remember is that you are the only person who is ever going to read what you write, so be honest and also know there is no wrong answer. If you run out of fears, then make something up and don't judge what you are writing or how you are writing it. Make sure you actually write the fears down on paper. This process is more powerful when you write by hand rather than typing on a computer, as the activity of handwriting more easily accesses the subconscious mind. You may also find it helpful to set a timer for 2-5 minutes so you know you have to write as quickly as you can.

1 Take a deep breath and remember to keep breathing.
2 Decide on your statement and begin writing.
  A fear I have about being born is_____
3 Write it down.
  Another fear about being born is_____
  Keep repeating the statement and writing down your fears until your time is up. If you feel like you are still flowing with ideas, keep going until you feel you have come to a natural end.

You may find your words flowing and that you are able to easily list them. If you find you are getting stuck, then keep writing the beginning of the sentence over and over until it flows again.

You will find your limiting beliefs that were created during the time of birth. If you are doing this is at the time of becoming a parent or giving birth, it will also highlight your most common limiting beliefs. Then you can use one of the methods above to identify where your ECHOs associated with the belief that was created. If you are working on your own birth experience, then you will be able to more easily imagine your baby self back at that time and have something to work with using EFT and Matrix Reimprinting.

Here is an example of my own process on being born. What I found fascinating is that I started off writing as if I was in the womb and then naturally transitioned to it being after birth. I saw too that my core beliefs were easily identified in this exercise.

- A fear I have about being born is that nobody will be there for me.
- Another fear about being born is that I'm going to get stuck.
- Another fear about being born is that I might not make it.
- Another fear about being born is that everything will change.
- Another fear about being born is that I will die.
- Another fear is I will do it wrong.
- Another fear about being born is they won't like me.
- Another fear about being born is it's not safe.
- A fear about being born is it's cold.
- A fear about being born is that it's too noisy.
- A fear about being born is that it smells horrible.
- A fear about being born is that I'm all alone.
- A fear about being born is that it's strange.
- A fear about being born is not being loved.

Remember to tap on anything that comes up using EFT or Matrix Reimprinting.

Now that we have explored in detail how beliefs are formed and imprints are created, in the next chapter we will begin to look at some of the specific issues that might come up during birth and pregnancy.

Chapter 15

# Dealing with Specific Pregnancy Issues

*Birth is not an emergency. It is simply an emergence.*
**Jeannine Parvati Baker**

Pregnancy is a time of heightened emotions. It can bring to the surface a whole range of emotions for the mother, and as a result, create a whole host of imprints for the child. In this chapter we will explore some of the issues that can arise as part of pregnancy and childbirth.

We'll also explore how the pace of the actual birth can affect our perception of ourselves and the world. During the latter half of the chapter we will look at the impact that fast and slow births have on the child, and the way the child shows up in the world.

## Issues that May Arise in Pregnancy

During pregnancy, many subconscious limiting beliefs will become heightened and many fears will come up. Here are some of the fears parents have shared with me and limiting beliefs that could be accompanying them.

| The Fear | Limiting Belief |
| --- | --- |
| Will I be a good enough mother? | I'm not good enough/I'll do it wrong |
| Will I be able to love them enough? | I'm incapable |
| Will he be taken from me, i.e. in an accident, or maybe he won't survive/thrive? | The world is a dangerous place |
| I'll let my baby down | I'm not good enough |
| I don't know what to expect | The world is a dangerous place/I'm not safe |
| I'm afraid of pain and I won't be able to cope | I'm a failure/not good enough |
| I'm afraid of giving birth (because of others' negative stories) | I'm powerless/I'm a victim/I'm not safe |
| Fear of the responsibility – one lady shared "How would I teach my baby to drink? I practically felt I needed to teach the baby to breathe…as if I had this HUGE responsibility to teach her all… Now she is 35, and breathing fine." | I'm not good enough/I'm incapable/the world is not safe |
| I'm afraid of being in hospital and feeling out of my control/comfort zone | I'm not safe/I'm not in control |
| I won't know how to look after a tiny baby (no experience/no user manual) | I'm not good enough/I'm incapable |
| Fear of PND (Postnatal Depression) | I'm powerless |
| Fear that something could happen to me or my partner: I had this heightened awareness of being vulnerable | The world is a dangerous place/I'm not good enough/I'm not safe |
| Fear of the danger in the world. News, wars, people taking other people's children. It made me more vigilant and protective | The world is a dangerous place/I'm not safe |
| I won't have support, nobody will help out | I'm alone |
| Fear of not conceiving | I'm not good enough/I'll get it wrong |
| Fear of not deserving a baby | I'm not good enough |

Many of these fears and limiting beliefs can be traced back to before the mother was six years old. Behind a fear there is normally a belief. (You can also refer back to the exercises on identifying limiting beliefs and naming your fears in Chapters 4 and 13, respectively.)

During pregnancy, there is a host of issues that may get spotlighted for the mother. She may have memories of her own birth, either conscious or subconscious. If, while the mother was in the womb, she had fears of being trapped there, these might manifest in different ways; she may, for example, feel fear that she is trapped by pregnancy.

Pregnant mothers often find that they have dreams about giving birth. Sometimes these dreams are representative of the way that they were born themselves. There is often a link with how we were born and the experience we have of giving birth.

Memories of sexual abuse are often brought up during pregnancy. Sexual abuse can be a cause of infertility, so getting pregnant in the first place may have taken time, and left the mother with feelings of shame, guilt and not being good enough. (Past sexual abuse can also affect the sperm count for the father.)

Some women may have blocked memories of abuse, which start to surface during pregnancy. For women that have been abused, having a baby growing inside them can trigger feelings of invasion and a lack of control. Women who have been abused may also get triggered into feelings of fierce protection for the baby, and anxiety about how they are going to keep it safe.

In *When Survivors Give Birth*, Penny Simkin and Phyllis Klaus highlight the effect that abuse can have on pregnant women.

In the mid-1980s in our work with childbearing women – Phyllis as a psychotherapist and counsellor and Penny as a childbirth educator, counsellor, and doula – we began to learn that women who have been sexually abused during childhood were often especially anxious during pregnancy, and frequently went through difficult or even traumatic experiences with birth and early parenting. They often could barely tolerate physical examinations and invasive procedures.

The unpredictability of labour and birth, the prospect of great pain, and an inability to control their own behaviour and labour process were especially troubling. These women had trouble trusting their doctors, midwives and nurses. They worried about their ability to be good parents.[91]

In addition, Simkin and Klaus state that "Women with prior mental health disturbances or a history of childhood sexual trauma seem particularly vulnerable to PTSD after childbirth."

Fear can slow down or halt the birthing process. It is a survival response that activates in order to allow the mother to find a safer place to give birth. In hospitals this is not an option, and what happens instead is that the hospitals administer drugs or other medical interventions to speed up the process, throwing the mind and emotions into conflict. I've found that the people who are affected the most are those who have already experienced Big-T trauma or had PTSD prior to giving birth – birth often retriggers a traumatic experience. We tend to think of PTSD as relating primarily to war issues, but it can occur after any severely traumatic incident.

Women who have been abused are also more prone to PND (or Postpartum Mood Disorder as it is known in the US) and can experience difficulty in bonding with their baby and breastfeeding. They may also have higher levels of anxiety, sleep problems, and be fearful of being alone with the baby. Sometimes they find themselves projecting their own fears onto the baby. In some cases, the mother may have fears about harming or molesting her baby, or that she will be a bad parent.

Grief can also be a strong emotion felt during pregnancy and around the time of childbirth. This grief can stem from not having felt loved and nurtured as a child, and can also be grief about the fact that life is changing.

If a pregnant woman has lost her mother, the grief around this might be heightened during pregnancy. During this time, women often experience a natural urge to have their own mother around more. If their mother is either dead or absent, or they don't have a good connection with her, then they may experience a deepening of the grief around these issues.

The father may be triggered by his own birth experience too. When carrying out the Matrix Birth Reimprinting work on any of the issues mentioned in this section, it is helpful, as a practitioner, if you can also include some work with the father. In an ideal world, it would be helpful if everyone attending the birth had cleared their own birth trauma.

## When the Mother has Previously Miscarried

Many women carry the grief of losing their children for the whole of their lives. The psychological effects of losing a baby are only recently being handled with care and sensitivity in hospitals.

### Josephine – Healing Grief

During the 1970s, Josephine experienced a stillbirth, followed by a miscarriage. The third time she got pregnant, she actually went on to have a beautiful healthy daughter, but unbeknownst to her, her father was in a different hospital, dying, whilst she was in labour. There was a lot of grief connected to all three pregnancies. We began with the stillbirth. I carefully guided her back into the memory asking, "Where do we need to start?" She began by explaining that as soon as her baby was born, it was taken away from her; she didn't get to hold, name, or even see it. She and her husband didn't get to say goodbye, so they felt that there was never any closure. This was a very common occurrence in hospitals at that time. She didn't have a funeral for her baby because the hospital took care of that, so she didn't even know what happened to her baby's body. I asked her to tap on her ECHO and her husband's ECHO for all that loss that they were both feeling at the time. We also worked on educating the doctors and nurses around her, and we asked the midwife to hand her the baby so she could hold him. I then asked her to create the most beautiful, sacred, happiest place that she could imagine, and she created this sacred place out in nature for herself and her husband. She named the baby Robin and then she buried his body in the ground of that place. She could also still see the spirit of the baby there in her arms. What was interesting was that the baby's spirit started to grow older, and it turned into a child of around 5 years old. The child started running around and they were able to play with him. Josephine knew that she had created a meeting place where they could come and play with their son. This was the picture we reimprinted and it brought her great peace.

During the next session, we did something similar with the miscarriage. We went back to the house where the miscarriage had happened. We cleared the grief of losing the baby and the trauma of everything that had happened around the miscarriage. She took the baby to the sacred place and she named him Simon. She buried his body right next to Robin's. Again, the spirit of the baby remained in her arms. He grew to about the age of three, and he started playing with his 5-year-old brother, so she now had two spirit babies, both playing in the sacred space. We reimprinted that picture.

In the third session, we visited the birth of her daughter. I asked Josephine this question: "If you had known that your father was dying, would you have wanted to be told and be with him?"

"Yes," she replied, "I would have wanted to have been told."

We stopped the birthing process, and Josephine gently told her ECHO that her father was gravely ill in the next hospital and they went to be him. At the hospital, she sat with her father and had a conversation with him, saying everything to him that she had wanted to say. She sat with him and held him while he died. We took her father's body to the sacred place and we buried his physical body next to the bodies of the two boys, whilst he stood next to her in his spirit form. Her father and the two boys started to play with her and her husband and celebrate being together. So when I asked her where she would like to give birth to her daughter, she said, "I'd like to give birth to my daughter in the sacred space." We changed the sacred space so it was accommodating for a baby's birth and she birthed her daughter into this sacred space in the presence of her husband, father and the two boys. She was able to relax and go through the bonding process with her daughter, and do it in a joyful way. She was no longer holding that grief for the two boys – it was just a beautiful picture, which we reimprinted.

The three sessions had a very powerful effect on her, and on her husband as well. She said after the session, "I can't tell you the difference it made to how I, and George, view the loss of our sons."

As mentioned before, a miscarriage can leave the imprint of death in the womb that is picked up by the child that follows. A close friend of mine spent many years speculating on the difference between her and her brother. While she had always been outgoing and positive, her brother was the polar opposite, and experienced many self-destructive tendencies, including serious addictions and thoughts of suicide. When she studied Matrix Birth Reimprinting, it occurred to her that there had been two miscarriages between her own birth and her brother's. There were many other environmental and social factors that could have impacted on her brother, such as a serious accident that her father had, just after her brother was born. However, she highlighted how she had often had the fear that she had "sucked all the joy out of the womb," before she learnt about the effects of miscarriage on the child that followed. Understanding this meant that she no longer felt responsible for her brother's mental state.

## 'Ben' – Mother Miscarried Previously, Causing Irrational Fear by Ted Wilmont

One of the first times I used the Matrix Birth Reimprinting process was with a 21-year-old client named Ben, who had an irrational fear of having a stroke. Ben had severe palpitations and a racing heart. He had been through all the tests and scans available, but cardiologists had told him, "You have a perfect and healthy heart."

Ben had been given Prozac. Before this, he had been very fit. He had been a runner, but he stopped running because he was scared it would bring on a heart attack.

I had an intuition that the feeling Ben had stemmed back to a birth issue. I instructed him to tune into the energy that he was feeling around this issue and then asked, "Did you feel like this before birth, during birth, or after birth?"

"It was before birth," he replied.

Ben knew the story of his birth. He knew that his mother had miscarried before him.

When he went back to what had happened at his birth, he revealed, "They gave me the last rites as soon as I was born."

"Why would they do that?" I questioned.

"Well, apparently my heart was really racing and they were really worried for me, so they called the priest to give me my last rites and baptise me."

Up until that point Ben had not made the connection between receiving his last rites because his heart was racing, and his anxiety about his physical condition.

We worked on Ben in the womb first of all. He said it was dark and horrible in the womb and that he was also born prematurely, which is why they were so worried about him. Basically, Ben felt he had left the womb early because he hadn't liked it in there. So we changed the colour of the womb and tapped on his mother's ECHO to calm her down. He said the colour changed to a lovely, healthy red colour.

> We reimprinted his birth, taking him out of fear and into calm.
>
> Ben rang me three weeks after that to tell me he had come off Prozac.

## When One Twin Dies in the Womb

When a twin dies in the womb, it can create a whole host of challenges for the twin that is left behind. This can include anything from guilt for surviving, fear of being left alone, right the way through to suicidal thoughts and tendencies. The following case study highlights some of these challenges:

> ### 'Robert' – When One Twin Dies in the Womb
> ### by Sally Ann Soulsby
>
> Sally carried out the following session with her client, Robert, who worked as a senior civil servant. Originally he came to therapy as he had thoughts of suicide, including planning in detail how he would kill himself. The only reason he had not carried this out was because he had two children of his own from a former marriage and couldn't bear to hurt them.
>
> Robert had experienced a strange death wish for as long as he could remember and this had led him to join the armed forces early on in life, where he had often fantasised he would be killed in action. A few months before the session, his girlfriend had died suddenly and he felt guilty he hadn't acted sooner to get her to hospital. We connected with the ECHO calling for the ambulance and tapped on the fear and confusion in his chest. The ECHO also had an acute fear of death and suddenly Robert began associating with his ECHO. He visibly shook in his chair. I helped Robert to return to the present moment and we carried out several rounds of EFT on his fear of death until he was calm.
>
> When we returned to the memory, he almost immediately went back to the womb where he and his twin brother, Paul, were about to be born. Robert started to drift in

and out of conscious awareness at this point.

He told me his twin, Paul, had died at birth and he could hear his brother speaking to him in his left ear. He was able to tap on his brother who, he discovered to his surprise, had been named after the doctor delivering them. He prepared Paul for what was about to happen and reassured him that he was loved. Robert's ECHO wanted to stay connected to his brother, so they created a signal they could use to communicate with one another whenever they wanted to. We then recreated their birth where adult Robert received baby Paul and held him in his arms. I left them together for some time so they could experience being connected after the birth.

Robert's old belief system was, "I want to follow my brother to the grave – I don't want to live without him." He could now understand why this feeling had haunted him all his life. Previously he had no idea that this incident was connected to the feeling he was having. Once he was able to connect with Paul, he no longer felt this belief to be true. He changed the belief to "I can live fully and joyfully, knowing I am always connected to Paul and I can live for both of us."

We reimprinted a new picture and checked on Robert's ECHO. He was in a completely different state of mind. He was relaxed and happy and no longer had the colic, which had afflicted him as a baby. After the session, Robert was very moved and relieved. His suicidal thoughts disappeared from that day. He often connects with Paul in the matrix.

### 'Steve' – Weight Loss

I was working with Steve on a weight loss issue. He was desperately trying to lose weight and no matter what he did, his weight stayed the same. We carried out a couple of sessions mainly around his weight, but nothing seemed to be working for him. During one of the sessions, he told me that he'd gone to see a hypnotist who had taken him back to being in the womb. He had realised that there was an empty space next to him in the womb where his twin had been.

We carried out a Matrix Reimprinting session, working with the energy of his brother that was left there and we reconnected him with his brother.

When we finished the session, he said to me, "Oh, my God! I've actually got a realisation that when I buy a birthday card for my mother, I buy her two cards. When I buy her a present, I buy her two presents. I may not always give her two cards or two presents, but I always buy two of everything. The other thing I do is, when I buy food, I buy two of everything. If I buy a pack of chewing gum, I buy two. If I buy a bottle of water, I buy two. If I buy a Mars bar, I buy two. If I buy a sandwich, then I buy two. I have just realised that not only am I trying to compensate for my twin not being here, but I'm also eating for two."

It was at that point that he was able to see what he was doing, and he was able to start dropping the weight. He realised that he didn't actually need to eat for two people. He only needed to eat for himself.

It's common for women to lose a twin during early pregnancy and not know that it happened, other than there is a little bleeding. At this time they worry they are losing the baby, have the scan and all is fine, and the scan shows only the one baby.[92]

### Twins in Utero

Ultrasound imaging clearly shows the interaction between twins in the womb. They can be seen repeatedly hitting, kicking, kissing, or playing together. A very strong bond is created between the two because they have shared these early experiences together. There may also be a dominant twin, and this twin continues to be dominant throughout their lives.

One story emphasizes the consciousness and connection between twins, as one twin helps the other to survive a life-threatening situation. An article from *The Daily Mail* describes how, at the 20-week scan, the doctors discovered that one twin, Kiki, had a heart problem, and fluid was leaking from her placenta. They told the mother that that twin would not survive. As they did the scan they watched in amazement as the second twin, Nico, sensing something was wrong, positioned herself low in the womb, plugging the leaking placenta and staying in a position that saved Kiki's life. They were born at 30 weeks and both are healthy little girls.[93]

## Premature Twins
Author Gregg Braden also shares a story of twins born prematurely. At a hospital where twins were routinely separated even if they were premature, the nurse could see that one of the babies was not doing very well and she suspected it was going to die. She broke protocol and placed the twins together in the incubator. The healthy twin put her arm around her twin and immediately her vital signs started to pick up.[94]

## Pre-conception Issues
If, during a Matrix Birth Reimprinting session, you go back to conception and there is still an issue, then it is likely that you are dealing with something that you brought in with you from a past life. In my experience, we tend to carry over past life issues if we didn't resolve them in a previous life. There are varying views about whether we should even concern ourselves with past life issues when we do this work. Some say that we have enough to deal with from this lifetime without going into past lives. However, I've worked with some people who have been trying to transform an issue for years or even decades, and it has only been by going into a past life that they were able to get to the root cause and get a solution. If it is affecting you in this lifetime, then it is important to go back there and get resolution.

However, I have also witnessed people who focus so much on their past life issues that they don't ever really clear anything in this lifetime.

If you are working on past life issues, it is also essential to work on the reverberations of that issue in this lifetime.

Also, we think of past lives as being in the past, but there is one argument that states that there is actually no linear time, so these past lives could be other lives that your soul is living presently. As you change things in your present life, you could also be affecting another aspect of your soul in other lifetimes and maybe even in other dimensions. This concept can be a big leap for our Western minds to make, but essentially, if we understand that this work is affecting our past, present and future, we begin to understand the importance of doing this work on a personal level.

You can use the classic Matrix Reimprinting technique to work on past life issues. If you follow the energy to a 'memory' of a past life, simply step into the picture and tap on the past life self as you would any other ECHO.

## Conceived of Rape

When a baby is conceived of rape, it obviously brings about a host of issues for both the mother and the child. In such cases, we can reimprint what occurred for the mother, as well as all the emotions that were projected onto the baby in the womb. The following case study is a prime example of how Matrix Birth Reimprinting can be used to rewrite a conception issue such as this.

During the 2011 Hay House "I Can Do It" conference in London, Karl Dawson was demonstrating a constricted breathing exercise. This exercise can often bring trauma to the surface as the breath and emotions are linked. One participant suddenly called out, "I'm actually in quite a lot of trouble." I was there in the capacity of emotional helper, and I had a particularly strong sense to work with her. As I led her away she told me, "I just want to warn you that when I'm triggered like this I often pass out." If you recall the five 'Fs' of trauma from Chapter 4 – fight, flight, freeze, fainting and fooling around – it was apparent to me that some trauma was likely to be involved, due to her tendency to faint.

She told me, "This is so big, I don't know that you can deal with it."

I reassured her that I had dealt with countless intense and traumatic cases, but she insisted, "Other people haven't been able to deal with it. I've been trying to clear this for over sixty years and nobody has been able to help."

It took some time to calm her down and earn her trust, and when she finally did tell her story, she revealed that she had been conceived of rape. She was a twin. Her mum tried to abort both her and her sister. Her sister had died, but she had survived. When she was born, she was neglected by her mother. In addition, she was really close to her sister, who was born a year later (and who, incidentally, she was attending the conference with). She had always had the sense that the soul of her aborted sister was reborn as her new sister a year later. (She was definitely not the first person I have worked with who has had a similar sense.) Also, her new sister was born out of incest. Her sister's father was the brother of her mother.

In the session, we enabled her ECHO to feel safe after the abortion. We reconnected her with her sister in the memory and told her that her sister was going to come back and be with her at a later date. Unsurprisingly, as we were working on connecting her with her sister in the session, her sister actually came out of the Matrix Reimprinting presentation, sat down and said, "Look, I have to be with my sister while you're doing this work." We also did some work clearing the abuse in her family line and helped her baby self to feel safer coming into the world.

When we reimprinted her birth, she said the only person that she would truly like to be there was Sai Baba. She asked if I knew who he was and it turned out that we had both had connections with him. Many people say he is God in human form.

When it came to the bonding, I was aware that we hadn't cleared any of her mother's issues – she reacted strongly when she was being put into her mother's arms. In the face of working with time constraints, she decided it was inappropriate for her to bond with her mother, but chose to bond with Sai Baba instead. She said, "Put me back in Baba's arms," and she looked into his eyes and bonded with him. I have to say that this session was probably one of the most powerful bonding sessions I've ever witnessed. She perceived herself to be bonding with God. An outstanding therapist herself, she had explored countless therapies and modalities because she was trying to get back her connection with God, but she had never really *felt* that connection until this session. She didn't need to connect and bond with her mum – she needed to connect with God, and God for her, in the human form, was Sai Baba.

When she returned to the conference, she was able to stand up in front of a group of 200 people and talk about how she had been conceived during rape and how her mum tried to abort her, without being triggered. She shared her joy at being bonded with God, bringing many people in the room to tears of joy.

## Clearing Issues around Pregnancy

Before you give birth, it is advisable to clear any of the issues you might have around being in utero with Matrix Birth Reimprinting. If you have strong issues such as those relating to abuse, it is highly recommended that you clear these with a Matrix Reimprinting, or Matrix Birth Reimprinting, practitioner.

Lee Ann's session in Chapter 10 of this book is a good example of using Matrix Birth Reimprinting to clear the past trauma for mother and baby before the next child is born. Remember, you want to clear all the trauma from conception and pregnancy before you reimprint the birth. It is essential that you clear the birth trauma for both the mother and the baby.

Now that we have explored some of the specific issues and traumatic challenges that may have occurred in the womb, or even before conception, in the next chapter we will look at how a range of challenges can manifest in childbirth.

# Chapter 16

# Dealing with Specific Childbirth Issues

*Childbirth is an experience in a woman's life that holds the power to transform her forever. Passing through these powerful gates in her own way, remembering all the generations of women who walk with her... She is never alone.* **Suzanne Arms**

Childbirth itself can bring on a whole host of issues, all of which can be reimprinted. In this chapter we will explore some of the challenges that the birthing experience can bring up. These include the pace of the birth, the baby being born a different sex to what the parents were hoping for, as well as breech babies and how to turn them, with Matrix Birth Reimprinting.

## Pace of the Birth

If the mother's birth was slow and drawn out, there is a strong chance that her baby's birth will be similar. Laura Shanley, author of *Unassisted Childbirth*, shared how, because she knew she had had a traumatic birth, she had to clear her own birth trauma and educate herself on how a natural birth should be. Following this, she had five natural home births during which she was either alone or with her family, using her intuitive birthing process.

When she gave birth to her second child, her husband and son were in the other room. With her third child, her husband was at the library and her sons were sleeping. Her 1-year-old daughter was with her when she had her fourth child, and with her fifth, her husband was down the hall and her other children were sleeping.

Sometimes the baby is born too slow or too fast. In her book *Immaculate Deception*, Suzanne Arms describes what happened at her own birth.

I was born in 1944, a time when hospital births had just been established as the norm in America. In the hospitals, labouring women were routinely drugged unconscious and often didn't wake up until a nurse brought their babies to them. Nurses were under strict orders to call the doctor only at the very end of labour, but it was imperative that he (virtually all doctors at the time were men) be there for the delivery – nurses were not allowed to deliver babies themselves. Women in those days often had their legs held or even tied together to keep them from delivering before the doctor came, and unknown numbers of babies were permanently brain-damaged from being forcibly held back.

Because I came faster than expected and my doctor was enjoying a night out, he did not come quickly enough. My mother was alone with the nurse, according to hospital policy. (Her own mother, a petite deaf woman from Russia, had actually been locked in a hospital room to go through labour alone during World War I, with the excuse that there was a shortage of nurses.) Although drugged, my mother was awake when I was born. When my head began to show and the doctor had not yet arrived, the nurse placed a sanitary napkin between my mother's legs and pressed my head back each time a contraction forced it out, until the doctor finally came and 'delivered' me.

It was routine to separate mothers and babies after birth in U.S. hospitals. Most mothers weren't conscious to be able to see and feel their babies emerge. When my mother first saw me, three days after I was born, she did as her doctor instructed and fed me formula from a bottle without attempting to put me to her breast. That was modern childbirth in 1944.[95]

When I worked with Suzanne using Matrix Birth Reimprinting, we spent time working with her baby self in the womb, clearing the fear and rage at being stuck and held back. We transformed both the feeling of being a victim of the situation and the belief that she was going to die. She revealed that her baby self felt like she had died a couple of times during that birthing process and that her birth was a threatening situation. Suzanne could see that her birth had set up a pattern of abuse for her throughout life. In her sessions, we helped her to not only transform the birth experience by clearing the trauma and transforming the beliefs – we also recreated a natural, unhindered, empowered birth experience and bonding with her mother.

She was also able to find the gift in what she went through. Suzanne has played a pivotal role in the campaign for natural birth and her book is a hard-hitting exploration of the Western birthing system. She realises that without these experiences in her life, she might not be so passionate about her campaign.

It is worth noting that not only was Suzanne's birth traumatic, but, as her description above lets us know, her mother's had been too. Suzanne's own experience of giving birth to her daughter had also been traumatic. This often occurs when a pattern of birth trauma is set up in the family. Like any family pattern, it can keep repeating itself until it is resolved. By rewriting the trauma with Matrix Birth Reimprinting, we are breaking the patterns around what has gone before, and creating generational healing in the family.

In the film *What Babies Want*, there is an interview with a man whose mother was giving birth to him at the side of the road. His father, in panic because he didn't know what to do, pushed the baby's head back inside his mother. In the interview the man said, "I really didn't want to come out the second time; I was ready and willing the first time, but the second time it was like it was too scary out there – they didn't want me, they had rejected me and I just wanted to stay there and die. That experience has had a profound experience on me all my life: my life has been one abandonment after another and I can trace it back all through my life – I felt abandoned then, and over and over again, since."

In the same documentary, a woman who was giving birth in the

210

back of a car reveals how she had the contraction to give birth to her daughter but instead of giving birth, she put her feet on either side of the car seats, making her body as tense as she possibly could in order to stop her baby coming out.

Both these instances highlight the fear and ignorance that we have about giving birth naturally. In these cases, the baby was forced to stay in the womb because of the conditioning around the belief that the baby has to be born in a hospital. We have cut off our natural instincts as a result of our conditioning.

## Easy Birth

Sometimes an easy birth that goes to plan can leave a person with a unique set of challenges. Those that have had an easy birth may find that same sense of ease being mirrored in life. They see people around them struggling and they think they should too. Sometimes they find themselves feeling unworthy or undeserving of an easy life. They may also have fears about life getting harder later, and that they will have no coping strategies in place. If they are people pleasers, they may find themselves falsely going into agreement with others around the belief that if you are not struggling, you are not living. Or if something is easily won, there is no achievement in it.[96]

## Wrong Sex Babies

Sometimes a baby is born 'the wrong sex'. This can be because the parents were expecting or had been told that the child would be a different sex than it turned out to be. Karl Dawson often shares how he and his wife were told by the sonographer, during a routine scan, that the baby was definitely going to be a boy; the woman even became defensive when they asked if she was sure. So when his daughter was born, Karl went into shock and exclaimed, "Oh no, my baby is deformed," thinking that there was something wrong with his son, as this was what he was expecting the baby to be. Once he heard the words "Congratulations, you have a daughter" from the midwife, he realised what had happened in his mind and was delighted. Karl said recently during a Matrix Reimprinting session with his teenage daughter that when she followed the energy of what she was currently feeling back to her birth, she found that at that moment she had looked at her father's face, seen the disappointment and created the belief that "I'm a disappointment". She easily gets upset if she thinks she has done something wrong. During the session they explained to her ECHO that Daddy was just shocked because he was expecting a boy and he loves her very much and is very happy she is a girl. They reimprinted a picture of Daddy welcoming her into the world as a girl.

In other cases, particularly when the parents want a different sexed child to the one that they have, it can leave the baby feeling not good enough or that they have let their parents down. This feeling often carries on far into adulthood.

A friend and I were doing a breakout session together on a course that we were attending. We'd been asked to choose a limiting belief that had some emotional charge for us from a list that we were presented with. When my friend went through the list, none of the beliefs had a negative charge to them, but one of them made her laugh. I understand that laughter can often cover up a deeper emotion, so I guided her to choose the belief that had made her laugh. The belief was 'My penis wasn't big enough!' Obviously this was a belief intended for a male participant, so I was curious to discover how it related to her. She said, "My father always wanted a boy. I've spent my life trying to be the boy that my father wanted."

The interesting thing was that she was stunningly beautiful. She had a tall, slender figure with natural blonde hair. However, she had always had her hair cut in a boyish style and worn masculine clothes.

She was also a very successful businesswoman running a number of businesses, and as we started to discuss this further, she discovered a link with how she was always looking for validation and approval from the men in business and also in her life.

We carried out a Matrix Birth Reimprinting session on her. During the session we went back to the time of her birth when her father found out he had a daughter, and helped her baby self see how much her father loved her, both then and in the future.

The next time I saw her, which was a few months later, she'd started growing her hair a little bit longer and wearing it in a more feminine style. She had also changed the way she dressed. Most notably, her relationships with her father and her male business partners and male friends had also radically transformed.

---

## 'Heather' – Feeling stuck in life

Heather was 63 years old and feeling very stuck in life. She had hit rock bottom and didn't really feel like she could trust herself to make the right decisions. She had been forced to sell her house and was living back home with her mother. All her life she struggled with relationships, felt like she didn't know who she was and felt like nobody ever supported her. Having lost her business two years before, she was feeling burnt out and unsure where to go in life. She had been suffering with depression and had recently come off her anti-depressant drugs.

When she tuned into her body, there was a lot of black energy in her chest. We originally thought we would go back to when she was 2 and a half years old and her sister was born, and all her mum's attention went to her sister. She had felt like she was unwanted during this time.

When the session began, however, we soon found ourselves further back, in the womb at the second trimester. Her baby self was feeling unloved and unwanted. I asked Heather if she could love her baby self and she felt a shift as she did. We then tuned into her mother and found that she was feeling frustrated and angry because she, herself, was not feeling loved and supported. We looked at her mother's heart and discovered it was small and closed, which made sense, as she had never felt loved by her own mother. When we asked what her mother needed, the resource of a pink rose was called for. (As we mentioned, pink heals separation and brings

---

in love.) We explained to her baby self that it wasn't personal and that her mother wasn't able to give love because she hadn't received it herself. We also found her mother to be resentful of her own younger sister, which is why she had wanted Heather to be a boy: another point of resentment. We cleared the sibling resentment in both Heather and her mum.

The other reason her mother had wanted a boy was to make her father happy. Again, this enabled Heather to see how it wasn't personal. Once Heather's mother had opened her heart, Heather's baby self felt safe to start screaming. When I asked why she felt she needed to scream, she said it was because she just wanted to be noticed and heard. Whilst Heather's baby self was screaming, I asked her adult self to talk to her mother and explain what her baby self needed from her. Her mother was able to connect and love her when she understood what was required and needed. Heather's baby self started to relax and feel safe, knowing that she was loved and wanted. Her mother's gift was to show her what it felt like not to be able to express love so she could find her way back to love.

Initially there was some hesitancy in trusting that her mother would, after the session, always be this way. Heather knew that some of the events that were to come later in life were also on a similar theme, so the session included rewriting some of these.

We visited Heather's 4-year-old self after her sister was born. Heather's father was too busy to give her any attention and this triggered her into feeling that she was unwanted. We worked with her father, who was feeling the pressure and responsibility of having to work harder to provide for a growing family. I suggested that Heather talk to her 4-year-old self and let her know why her father was feeling that way. When her younger self understood that, again, it wasn't personal, she responded by getting up and skipping off to the garden.

Along the same theme, we visited Heather's 2-and-a-half-year-old self who was staying with her neighbour whilst Heather's sister was being born. Heather had had an accident while she was alone in the garden, falling off the swing and onto the concrete, breaking her front teeth. She was feeling alone and unloved, and she made the decision that, as nobody was going to be there for her, she would have to take care of herself, by herself. We tapped and released the shock of falling off the swing and Heather gave her younger self a hug. We brought her mother into the picture too.

When we checked back to see what we had done, her baby self was sleeping in the womb, feeling safe, loved and wanted. We reimprinted this picture using turquoise (the colour of trust and faith, which heals not being heard or being able to speak out).

Heather had spent her life not expressing her emotions as she was told, first, that she was not allowed to, and second, that she was unwanted when she did express her needs.

After the session, her depression dissipated, and she found a new, deeper and closer connection with her mother.

## Cord Around the Neck

Around a third of babies are born with the umbilical cord around their necks.[97] During the birthing process, the top of the uterus, placenta and cord all move down together. The uterus shrinks down, contracting and moving the baby downwards, along with the placenta and its attached umbilical cord. It's not until the baby's head moves into the vagina that a few extra centimetres of additional length are required.[98]

The cord will usually stay loose and flexible so the blood and oxygen can still move freely through it. But occasionally the cord will become stretched and tight during the last part of labour, as the head is coming out. This is when there is a short-term reduced oxygen supply through the cord and the baby feels the tightening of the cord around the neck. If the cord is loosened rather than cut at this point, it will return to full blood supply and the baby will physically recover quickly.[99]

The baby does not need to be able to breathe air whilst it is being born and only takes its first breath once its body is completely out in the air. That is why water births are safe for babies as the reflex to breathe is not triggered until out in the air.

However, getting stuck in the birth canal because the cord is too short and tightens can leave the baby feeling trapped. The cord wrapped around the neck can create an unconscious feeling of suffocation. Often, later in life, this manifests as panic when it seems that there is not enough air. It also manifests in the form of not being able to wear tight clothing around the neck and fear of being confined. There may be a tendency to worry about events before they happen because they seem life-threatening. These people could also feel a disconnection between the heart and the head and have difficulty expressing their feelings.[100]

If they had the cord around their neck and they were actually trapped because the cord was wrapped around their neck so tightly that they couldn't carry on descending, as adults, they often have a trapped feeling and get claustrophobic in tight spaces.

**Depression and Anxiety**
**by Forrest Samnik**

I carried out a Matrix Birth Reimprinting session with a client who had been taking Clonopyn and Seraquil – drugs for depression and anxiety. He was born with the umbilical cord wrapped around his neck. When we came to reimprinting the memory, he chose to have an angel hugging him while she gently loosened the cord from around his neck. He was able to let go of the sense that "My life is being squeezed out of me to the point I cannot breathe."

As an aside, having since carried out a number of these sessions where the cord was wrapped around the neck of the ECHO, I have discovered the importance of asking the client how they would like to resolve the issue of the cord. Some will want somebody else to help them, just as in the case study above. But others will choose to unwrap the cord themselves, creating a feeling of empowerment rather than feeling like a victim who needs to be rescued. Just before we start the Matrix Birth Reimprinting process, I will often ask the ECHO what they need in order to trust that the cord will stay away from their neck. Some will choose to hold the cord, others have chosen to have the cord on a hosepipe reel and have it easily unroll as they come out. Finding a way to create that extra bit of safety for them is often essential for taking them out of fear and into safety.

### Future Matrix Birth Reimprinting

In the previous chapter, it was suggested that any trauma around conception and being in utero needs to be cleared before the birth; the same applies to any birth trauma that the mother may have experienced. This includes any fear she has around giving birth. The Future Matrix Birth Reimprinting process is the ideal way to enable the mother to address her fears. Once you have done this, you can ask the mother to check in with the baby and see if there is anything they need to clear before they are born. This will enable the child to clear any issue or theme they may have been coming in with from a previous lifetime, and also anything that may have occurred in the womb. In order to carry out this process, the mother can visualize the baby and work with them as with an ECHO in Matrix Reimprinting. She can check and see how the baby is feeling.

Another technique I use with pregnant women is to ask them to check in with their body and womb, especially if they're not far from giving birth. Their body needs to be as relaxed as possible. Perhaps they are feeling tightness in their lower back, or there may be something going on with the ligaments, which need to be getting softer to allow the pelvis to move and open a bit more for the baby to come out. Ask the mother to check in with her body to see if there are any parts where she's holding tension, and then go in and clear that tension. You can ask her, for instance, if there is stiffness in her hips. You can ask her to imagine shining a light into this area and describe what that stiffness looks like, what it feels like, what colour it is, if it has any shape to it, and if there is an emotion stuck in there. Metaphor work is very powerful in this instance. Work with whatever comes up to resolve the issue inside the body, using EFT tapping.

Once the body feels like it is relaxed and ready to give birth, the next step is to get the mother to explain to the baby that the birth is not happening now, but it is going to be happening in the future.

Next, ask the mother to set up her birthing room: what will she need in order to feel empowered and able to be in her body? Ensure she has all the resources that she needs.

Next, guide the mother through the birthing process and bonding process, sending the new picture out.

### Starting Labour and Turning Breech Babies

You can use Future Matrix Birth Reimprinting to stimulate labour or help to turn the baby if they are breeched. In most cases, fear stops the baby from coming out or being in the right position.

If the labour isn't starting, or the baby is in breech, assuming that it isn't an emergency, you can intervene with the process. In most cases, both the mother and the baby will be feeling pressure for the delivery to be on time. They may also be afraid that the birth is not going to go well, or that the process is going to be taken out of their hands. There is nearly always an issue of safety. The baby picks up on its mother's fears and does all it can to stay in the womb until she is feeling safer.

Use EFT to tap on the fears and allow the mother to express and feel that fear and use Matrix Reimprinting to work on the baby in utero to release the fear the baby is picking up.

---

#### 'Amy' – Avoiding Induction and Possible C-section

Amy called me at 10 p.m. because she was in fear. The doctors had told her that her baby was overdue and was breeched. She was told that if the situation didn't rectify itself in the next two days, they would bring her in to be induced and there

---

might be a C-section. We worked on the pressure she felt and the fear that the birthing process was going to be taken over by the doctors. We also connected with the baby to see how she was. Not surprisingly, the baby was feeling her mother's fear and didn't want to come out. She felt it wasn't safe to do so, so we tapped on these emotions. As we were working, Amy felt her baby turn in the womb and at 2 a.m. that night, she went into labour and had a natural birth.

When we practice Future Matrix Birth Reimprinting, the changes happen on a number of levels. On a very basic level, if we look at NLP and a process known as modelling, we are rehearsing how we want the birth to go, and creating new neural connections in the brain about our expectations of the birth. The way we anticipate the birth can have a profound effect on how it turns out.

However, with this process we are affecting far more than the mind-body connection. We are also affecting the energetic field associated with the birth. The energy that has been created from fears, past experiences, stories from others and previous birth traumas is stored in the field or matrix. We keep tuning into it and it influences the birth itself. When we reimprint a new, positive picture in the field, particularly if we tune into it with our thoughts, feelings and emotions, it creates a strong resonance towards the positive birthing experience. Karl Dawson states that these new, positive pictures have a much higher resonance than the negative pictures. When we replace them, we tune into the field of the positive birth. And when the birthing process commences, that is the picture that we tune into. We take the information into our bodies that this is the way it is going to go, and our bodies respond accordingly.

Now that we have explored how you can reimprint issues from childbirth, in the next chapter we are going to look at how, when we reimprint the birth after the baby is born, it can have an effect on the way the child shows up in the world.

# Chapter 17

## Working on the Mother After Birth

*Forgiving is for giving yourself the freedom to be happy again.*
**Stephen Lane Taylor**

One of the most potent discoveries that I made with the Matrix Birth Reimprinting protocol was that if we work with mothers to reimprint the birth of their baby after it is born, it can have a profound effect on the child's physical and emotional health.

When we do this work, it is taking place on a quantum level, beyond the limited perception of the conscious mind. There is an energetic field around the birth, containing all the information of the birth, including the mother's attitudes, beliefs and projections. When these are cleared and healed, it can change the connection between the mother and the child. The following case studies are classic examples of how this can play out.

> ### Jake – Reducing the Effects of Epilepsy
> I worked on Meggie, and surrogately on her son Jake, who was seven years old at the time of these sessions.
>
> Jake had epileptic fits 2 to 3 times a day. He had experienced these fits since birth. I asked his mother to explain to me a little bit about what happened while she was pregnant with Jake and whether there were any big traumas that happened then. She replied, "Absolutely. I was six weeks pregnant when I found out. I told my husband and he was absolutely delighted. He seemed to be so excited that we

were having a child. For two weeks we talked about it and got excited together and then one day he didn't come home from work." She didn't know whether he was alive or dead for some time. He had literally vanished off the face of the earth. He didn't reappear until a week after Jake was born. He had left out of fear of being a father.

During the first session we actually worked on the trauma of his disappearance. We used Matrix Reimprinting to work on her younger self and the feelings of shock, confusion, grief, and not knowing if he was dead or alive. We tapped on baby Jake in the womb as well. We released all the shock and trauma that he was feeling, that he was picking up from his mum and making his own. We worked surrogately on Meggie's husband. Meggie is highly intuitive and she was able to connect to her husband's 7-year-old ECHO who had made some decision that he couldn't be a father, and that he couldn't be responsible for a child. She then worked surrogately with her husband and got the understanding of why he left when he did. This was immensely healing to her because he never really explained to her why he had done so; he may not even have understood himself that it was connected to something that happened when he was seven years old. We reimprinted the picture of Meggie, her husband and his 7-year-old self all together.

At the end of this session Meggie asked me whether she should tell her husband about the session we'd just done. I left it up to her. She called me the next day. "You'll never guess what. My husband came home from work and before I could even tell him what we had done in the session he said, 'I suddenly felt emotional today and I had to go into the toilets and cry. I've got no idea where the emotion came from but I feel great now.'"

"What time was that?" Meggie asked. It happened at the time of our session – something that I have experienced on many occasions. And so Meggie told him about the session.

After the first session, Jake's fits reduced from 2-3 times a day to once a week.

In the second session, we worked on Jake's birth, which was highly traumatic. There was a high level of medical intervention and Jake was not breathing when he was born. He almost died. He had to have numerous operations, had all sorts of cannulas put into him and had tubes coming out of every orifice. We cleared the trauma of Jake's birth as well as that of the medical intervention. We reimprinted his birth, including the bonding with his mum. There were numerous angels called in to help him during the reimprinting session.

Something unexpected occurred after the session. That evening, Jake had a very intense fit. Meggie described it as the worst fit that he had ever experienced. She said that during that fit he started bringing up black liquid; she instinctively knew that he was discharging all the medication he'd been given. Meggie said that even though it was an intense fit, and usually following a fit he would go to sleep, he was actually full of energy afterwards. He looked at his mum and said, "Oh, thank you, Mummy." She cleaned him up and he went about his day, carrying on playing.

Following that second session, he went a whole month without a fit. In addition, his schoolwork started to improve. He started getting gold stars and achievement awards. He started to get commendations for helping others and his reading and writing began to improve.

In the third session that we did together, we worked on Meggie's fear of taking him out on his own. She feared taking him out alone because she was concerned that he was going to have a fit. She felt that she couldn't cope with people staring, and nobody ever helped her when he did have a fit in public. When we were reimprinting one of her previous memories of Jake having a fit in public, I asked her to stand back and look at herself and how other people saw her. She realised that the reason that nobody had helped was because other people saw her as being in control of the situation. She also saw how other people were going into their own shock and trauma of actually seeing this little boy having a fit, and that they often felt unable to help. I asked her if there was anybody who had ever helped her and she said, "Yes, there was one guy that came along and scooped him up in his arms when he'd finished fitting and carried him back to the car for me." In the reimprint we asked that guy to come in and give a job to each of the people watching and to explain to them that although Meggie looked really confident, she actually needed help.

After the third session, Jake went four months without a fit.

Jake had a Vagal Nerve Stimulator (VNS) implanted in his chest when he was about two years old. VNS therapy uses a pulse generator to send mild electrical stimulations to the vagus nerve with the aim of reducing the number, length and severity of seizures.[72]

His doctors began wondering why he was suddenly able to go for months without a fit. During those four months, Meggie became pregnant with Jake's brother. She told me that although she had wanted another child, she could never have imagined having one when Jake was having so many fits each day. Previously there had been no space in her life for any child other than Jake.

In 2014, Jake was 13 years old and, on average, having a fit only every three months.

### 'Claire' – Angry Conception and Birth of her Daughter In Her Own Words

I worked with Sharon on my daughter's birth. The session took place when my daughter was 2 and a half. I had always had mixed feelings about her birth, and it brought up emotions of both joy and sadness.

When I worked with Sharon, I thought we would begin with the birth itself, but actually we went back before that to a memory where I was in a restaurant with my parents and my brother. My mother was telling me, "Stop holding your stomach, stop being so silly, you're only seven weeks pregnant." I asked her why I should stop holding it and she replied, "What if you miscarry? Come on, stop being silly. Nobody holds their tummy like that at seven weeks." I remember being angry and protective over my baby, and also feeling fear at what she had said. Sharon asked me how much of that fear was mine and how much of it was my mother's. It was 90% hers. She had suffered a very traumatic miscarriage 30 years previously. I realised that I took on my mother's fears that day. I squashed them down and tried to push through it for the next seven months, but they resurfaced as soon as the pain started in labour. We released these fears in the session.

Next, we went to the moment my daughter was conceived. Ren, my partner at the time, and I had both been angry when she was conceived and we weren't even looking at each other during that moment. Sharon asked me, "How much of that is anger, and how much is passion?" I looked again. I started to laugh. With me it was 90% anger and 10% passion. With Ren it was 10% anger and 90% passion! No wonder he had always looked so confused when I said that our daughter was created in anger. He had always said: "I don't remember being angry!" In the session, we changed the picture so that he and I were facing each other, and much of the anger resolved for me.

Next we reimprinted my labour. I was crouched, leaning over my bed and Ren was sorting through the hypnobirthing scripts. As the pain got more intense, I asked him, as my birth partner, to take control. That was his designated job so that I didn't have to be in charge of anything but releasing my body. I waited for him to step into place and when I looked up, he seemed panicked and anxious. This set my heart pounding straight away.

"I don't know where to…"

I cut him off. "Have you read it all twice? Like you said you would?"

"No, not twice, but…"

I cut him off. "Do you know the scripts off by heart?"

"No, but…"

"*Get out!* If you are not here for me, then I have to do this alone," I shouted.

I was in fight or flight and flooded with adrenaline. Our baby was stopped in her tracks at that moment.

In the session, I froze Ren at the door before he left. I took the time I needed to come back to myself and to step out of fight or flight. We brought in colours to ease the fear. I began to realise that everything could still be perfect, even if it was not how I had hoped it would be. Throughout this process, Sharon was either tapping on my finger points or holding my hand. It anchored me. I began to realise that my partner had been scared too. Scared of getting it wrong and of me being in pain, and of being in charge of guiding his baby into this world. I realise how he must have felt to be sent out of the room. In the session I unfroze him and stopped him at the door, saying, "I'm calm now. Don't go. What were you about to say?" He looked relieved and came back in.

"I was going to say that I wasn't sure which script you'd like to start with. Not that I didn't know anything."

At this point, Sharon wanted to check in with my daughter's ECHO. She was anxious, but beginning to feel better. We sent her some colour, but she didn't need to be tapped on. She wanted me and her father to kiss and hug.

We changed my bed to a birthing pool and this time we were all in it together. My 'present self' was called in to be the midwife. Sharon guided me through as I started to birth our baby, but then she left me to experience the rest in silence. This was such a gift. I breathed and felt the waves start to push through me. I felt my daughter start to descend and crown.

When I came to rebirth her I realised that my daughter was coming out feet first. Instead of panicking, I thought to myself: "Typical of her, getting her feet out first so she could 'hit the floor running' in her own unique way." It also meant that her shoulders didn't get stuck, which is what had happened when she was actually born. This time around, 'midwife me' caught her perfectly under the water and handed her to me; she immediately started to suckle and feed. I could actually feel the tugging on my nipple as I experienced this. I looked into my daughter's eyes and she into mine. I reached up and wrapped my hand around Ren's neck. He kissed me on the shoulder. "Thank you," he said. And I felt his strength and his arms around us both. I said out loud to Sharon: "I can 'hold' them both at the same time." That was a belief change for sure. I had always felt that I only had enough in me for her, not enough love and patience and time for both of them. Ren looked into his baby's eyes and they bonded and then we settled down together. The sunrise was shining through the windows of our bedroom and everything was gold and pink and orange. This was the image that we reimprinted. This was my daughter's new birth.

That night I went back to the hotel where Ren was looking after our daughter. Even though we are no longer in a romantic relationship he remarked over dinner that I kept looking at him 'passionately'.

Back in the room, my daughter and I decided to have a bath together as we so often do before bed. I was halfway through washing my hair when Ren knocked on the door and asked if he could come in. We're still pretty close and he has seen me naked a thousand times, so I said yes. He came in and our daughter started asking him to get in the bath with us. "All together, all together," she kept saying. We both tried to tell her that the bath was too small and that Daddy had already had a shower and other such things to dissuade her, but she was having none of it. "I don't mind," I heard myself saying!!!!!!

"Urrrm, OK, I suppose," he said slightly hesitantly, and got in the bath behind me. I shuffled up but we were all leaning on each other. He had to rinse my hair with a cup because there was no room for me to lean back and rinse it. I froze and then smiled: we were in the exact same position we had been in the birthing pool!

The next morning, I woke up early and looked over to the twin bed on the other side of the room. My ex was awake too. In that hazy way you do, when you haven't totally woken up, I went over to him and said: "Hey, I know why I was looking at you like that yesterday. It was because I had sex with you in the matrix!" He was pretty shocked! But then we both began to laugh and I explained to him what I meant: that I had changed how we had conceived our daughter. We kept laughing and trying not to wake our little girl.

"I told you that I never thought she was made in anger," he said.

We both lay down next to our daughter to watch her wake up. He leant over and kissed my shoulder, just as he had done in the session. I didn't say anything. I kept that just for me.

### Bettina – Matrix Birth Reimprinting presentation at AMT's 2014 EFT Conference

I recently attended your Matrix Birth Reimprinting presentation at the AMT's EFT conference. I did not raise my hand when you asked who had had a traumatic birth. But, as you started describing what infants go through – the drops, the needles, the poking and prodding – I soon realised that my baby's birth was far from ideal. I started tapping along with tearful release. At one point I even considered leaving the room because I was so uncomfortable, but my inner voice told me to stay with it. I reimprinted my daughter's birth as you presented, tapping to clear the trauma at each point. By the time your presentation ended, all the dread had left me and I remember feeling a sense of peace.

Later that evening, I received a message from my 17-year-old daughter. She was in the United States at the time and did not know I was at the AMT's EFT conference. I had actually been trying to reach her for three weeks prior to that, but to no avail. In her message she wrote, "Whatever you did for me today, thank you. And for whatever happened between us, I forgive you. For the first time in my life I feel true joy. I know this is thanks to you."

You can imagine my amazement reading these words.

Having explored how transforming the mother's issues can have a profound effect on the way the child shows up in the world, in the next chapter we will explore fathers.

# Chapter 18

# Fathers Need Help Too

*The transition to fatherhood is one of the most significant and challenging experiences a man will ever face. In order to have a satisfying and successful experience, fathers must feel safe, supported and confident. To optimise the possibilities for our families, we need to provide appropriate educational, physical and emotional support for 'father love'.* **Patrick M. Houser**

The father plays a very important role in creating a strong and bonded family unit. As we highlighted earlier, if the mother is feeling loved and secure in her relationship, then she is more likely to have a peaceful baby who also feels loved and safe. If the father is fearful, angry and acts in a non-supportive or abusive way, the baby will pick up on these emotions through the mother.

### Becoming a Father

As we have seen in Meggie and Jake's story in Chapter 17, her partner went into shock when he found he was going to be a father. His past beliefs around being a father were triggered; the triggering was powerful enough to send him into the flight response.

During their partner's pregnancy, a father can also be consciously or unconsciously triggered by his experience of his own birth and childhood memories of how he was parented. These can be brought up to the surface, and fear can be created, particularly if he does not want to repeat patterns from his own father.

Other more practical concerns a father may have can include:

1 Responsibilities in providing for the family
2 Losing out on sleep and worrying that that will affect his work. As the provider for his new family, this can create stress and worry
3 Relationship with his wife or partner may change
4 Worrying if the baby will be healthy or not
5 Worrying about losing his partner or baby in childbirth

In addition, fears can arise that he will not be good enough or he will not know what to do to be a good dad.

## The Birth Process

Fathers are often forgotten in the birthing process, as all the attention is normally on the mother and the baby. However, they do experience the birth of their children in a very profound and powerful way that can affect the whole family unit.

Some of the concerns a father may have during the birthing process can include:

1 Feeling powerless and out of control as it is something outside of his perception. A man's common reaction to seeing his partner in pain is to want to 'fix' the situation and he gets frustrated because there is nothing he can do to fix it.
2 Feeling that this is an unsafe situation, especially as he has no idea how long the process is going to take.
3 Feeling shocked by the loud and unusual sounds that his partner is making. It can trigger a primal fear in him.

Sometimes fathers project anger at the other men or women who seem to be causing the mother of their child pain during the medical procedures, and if they are not able to express this anger, it will be internalised and held. Anger can also be triggered when information and knowledge they need is not shared with them by medical professionals.

Fathers can feel very left out of the whole experience and sometimes they feel unwelcome. There can be fear around not knowing what is happening and confusion around what is normal or what is supposed to be happening. Having a doula or an understanding, supportive midwife at the birth to reassure both the mother and the father creates a safer birthing environment.

## Should Fathers be Present at the Birth?

Patrick Houser, a natural birth educator and author of *The Fathers-To-Be Handbook* and co-founder of Fathers-To-Be, says that "research shows that hormonal activity in a father is altered during his partner's pregnancy, and more so if he is present at the birth. Hormones are chemicals secreted by an endocrine gland or some nerve cells that regulate the function of a specific tissue or organ. It is essentially a chemical messenger that transports a signal from one cell to another. In a way, they tell us what to do; how to 'act'. Prolactin, vasopressin and oxytocin are among the hormones that are found at higher levels in men around the time of birth. Increased production of prolactin is known to promote bonding/attachment and caring. Raised vasopressin levels cause a man to want to protect his family and be at home rather than 'on the prowl in search of a mate'. Vasopressin is also known as the monogamy hormone: commitment. Also if a father is intimate with his child, especially through skin-to-skin contact, his oxytocin production increases. Elevated oxytocin in a father is recognised as a key component in jump-starting and maintaining his nurturing instincts. In addition, a man in close contact with his child will have reduced levels of testosterone thereby causing him to be more gentle and relaxed, less likely to harm them and less likely to seek divorce."[102]

So not only does pregnancy and birth affect the mother's and baby's hormonal systems: the father's is affected too. Nature has given us human beings the best start possible for a healthy, secure family. All we have to do is to provide the safe and secure environment for the family unit to bond.

When it comes to working with fathers using Matrix Birth

Reimprinting, we can enable them to release some of the underlying fears that a man has traditionally been taught to brave through. Do you remember Lee Ann's session in Chapter 10 where we helped her to transform the memory of having a traumatic C-section and we then went on to have an empowered second birth experience? The following is a session with her husband Joel, showing his perspective on what happened to her, and how clearing it helped him to release the trauma of his first daughter's birth.

### Joel: A Father's Experience of a Traumatic Birth

When Joel found out they were going to have a second baby, he was really happy and both he and Lee Ann were celebrating; but in the back of both their minds, there was still the fear of having to go through another terrifying birth experience.

Joel told me that, "The experience of Lyla's birth took something away from me that I will never get back again. Even with the second one, it's not the same; every baby and every birth is different and I'll never get that back, so I was very angry. Obviously we talked about the possibility of taking legal action, but at the same time we wanted to enjoy the birth of the baby. We didn't want to go into legal action and get attorneys and start a whole process when we'd just had a baby. But I had a lot of emotions – I was sad and angry. Most of it was anger and frustration because I didn't know what I could have done differently."

We started the session using EFT and working on his feelings of anger, sadness and the feeling of powerlessness to be able to help Lee Ann. He also needed to spend some time releasing the shock he was feeling. Once the levels of emotion had come down we were able to step into the memory in the matrix and go right to the beginning of the labour when they broke Lee Ann's waters and started induction. Joel could see that at the time he had been feeling impatient and was wondering what was going on. He was holding all the impatience as tension at the back of his neck, so we tapped with his ECHO to release this tension and to also reassure him that this daughter was going to be fine.

Joel started to laugh as he watched himself trying to make Lee Ann laugh by making jokes to relax her. He said, "Some of the time she is laughing and some of the time she wants to punch me. But she is a strong girl and she is going with the flow and hanging in there."

We then moved to about 18 hours into the labour and Joel could see that he was getting impatient, angry and worried because he had been told that they only had 24 hours after they broke the waters for the baby to be born. After that, there would be danger of infection and he knew the dilation was not progressing as quickly as it should. The clock was ticking. His other fear was the uncertainty of it all. He had no idea how the process should be happening. He said, "You're not angry at the baby of course, you're just waiting and waiting and you are tired, physically tired, mentally drained. But I was also feeling helpless because it was something that I couldn't control – Lee Ann and I didn't want to go through the C-section process." As we tapped on Joel's ECHO and I asked what he needed, Joel said, "I'm going to tell Joel back then to be patient and strong – especially mentally strong..."

He added that he was feeling happier about the second birth because they had both done more research into natural birthing, and hired a doula and a really good obstetrician who had a high success rate for vaginal births after C-section (VBAC). I asked him to share all the knowledge he had gained with his younger self, and also to tell him that he has a healthy and beautiful little girl.

We were then able to move onto the C-section event. I asked Joel if there was anything he could tell his younger self to prewarn him of what was about to happen so he wouldn't be so shocked. Joel said, "Yeah, if I could go there right now, it will truly help me and prepare me mentally that what I'm about to experience is going to be a very steep roller coaster but it's going to be OK." He also wanted to reassure Lee Ann about it and told her, "There's going to be turbulence and the plane ride is going to be tricky, but we are going to land safely." As he did this, he saw her start to relax more.

It was then time to tune into baby Lyla and see how she was doing. He could sense that Lyla was also scared and as we tapped on her, he told her, "Daddy's about to see you and we're going to have so much fun and I can't wait to see you. Just hang in there, because it's just a matter of time, but we're going to take you home." She started kicking and moving around and was ready to come out into the world.

It felt like a really good place to stop and reimprint this picture as it was so powerful and filled with happiness. We did so. Joel could still sense the impatience, but he realised it was excitement rather than fear-based worry.

We then went on to visit the moment when the doctors came in and advised them to have the C-section. He described feeling "bombed". I asked him whether, with all the knowledge and understanding he has now, he thought they'd made the right choice together to agree to the C-section.

"Kind of fifty-fifty and let me explain why. The right choice, because regardless of how it happened, Lyla is healthy and she's out and she's running and she's happy and she yells and she screams and she's great. And no, because now that I know we could have waited longer, and I know that probably the doctor just wanted to be done – you know, get out and go home as he had a concert to go to. We could have waited longer, but I live with that decision because my daughter is healthy."

I asked, "And at that time were you both doing the best

234

you could? With all the knowledge and understanding that you had that time, forgetting what you know right now, with all the knowledge and understanding that Joel had at that time, was he doing his best?"

Joel replied, "At that time, yes. Not knowing what I know now, yes. At that time what I cared about was that the baby be safe and healthy, and that Lee Ann be safe and healthy." I asked him again, "Did you make the right decision to go ahead with the C-section?" He said that he did, and he forgave himself as he was doing the best he could.

We moved on to the time the doctors were prepping Lee Ann for the C-section and Joel was asked to step outside the operating room. Joel said, "I can see that as I was waiting, I was sad that it couldn't happen the way we wanted, but I was happy because I was minutes away from seeing Lyla."

A reminder here: although Lee Ann had had an epidural which was supposed to numb the lower half of her body, it didn't work, so she could feel everything they were doing to her to get Lyla out.

We did a little work with Joel's ECHO to clear the sadness and disappointment and then I did a little work with Joel himself to prepare him for working on the next part of the birth story – when his ECHO had returned to the operating room – so that he felt balanced in himself. Joel explained that as he stepped into that memory of being in the operating room, he could see that his ECHO had many emotions going on as Lee Ann was yelling and screaming and he was looking at the blood pressure equipment. Her blood pressure was so high that he felt like they were killing her. "I was holding her hand. I put my head down and I started crying because I had no idea what was going to happen. I remember I felt the nurse rubbing my back and I heard her saying, "It's going to be OK, it's going to be OK." I was speechless – I was in shock. I talked to Lee Ann at the beginning but there was so much pain that neither of us could focus and I didn't even know what to say, because I'd never seen a human being, and especially somebody that I love, go through that type of pain."

We spent time working on Joel, Lee Ann, Lyla and even the hospital staff for all the shock they were experiencing. Joel chose to bring in orange energy to give everybody strength. As a colour therapist, I know that orange is a colour that heals trauma and is also a colour for empowerment.

Joel then went on to say, "Lee Ann had made her choice. She did not want to be completely put under and anaesthetised until she heard Lyla cry and know that she was OK. I knew that there had been a choice and I honoured Lee Ann for her strength and courage even though she chose the hardest way. She is a great mom and it was at that point I realised how good a mom she was going to be. She is amazing and now I'm getting a lot of positive feelings – it was a weird and great experience because it made us a lot stronger. And I don't think I would have ever seen it that way until this point. That's how I feel right now: that it was all worth it, and we were put in a great situation to appreciate our daughter, for me to appreciate my wife even more as a woman, as a wife, as a mother and as a person. You know? How much can a human being go through?

Having options and taking the hard way out, I mean I wish that you could have been there in that room and seen what I saw, heard what I heard, like all the yelling and screaming. Whenever I looked at Lee Ann's heart rate monitor, her heartbeat was going so fast that you'd think that something terrible was going to happen and she went through all that as an option and she did OK, she did great. She got out healthy and so did Lyla, and I feel so much better.

I had a guilt feeling that I should have said this, I should have done that, or said something to the doctor, but you know, it was her decision most of it and I supported and

I suggested and I was on board, but ultimately it was her body and I have to respect that more than anything. Even though I'm Lyla's father, it was Lee Ann's body and it was her decision more than mine. We could have waited for a natural birth and we didn't; she could have been put to sleep but she didn't want that. And for two and a half years, I've had that feeling that 'it's my fault for not stepping up', but knowing now that we had options – I never saw it as though we had options – I always saw it as though we were pulled into this situation and I'm supposed to be the captain. Now I feel a lot different. Everything feels OK, now that I've come to terms that it wasn't my fault. I'm kind of ready – not to put everything behind and never revisit that place – but I'm ready to revisit that place with a different attitude, knowing that it wasn't my fault."

Joel's session shows how the fears and vulnerabilities that men face in childbirth can also be addressed and transformed. It is vital that men be included, and not overlooked, as we address the issues associated with birth trauma. Joel told me after the session that if he had done Matrix Reimprinting in advance, and had integrated his own life experiences, he would have felt safer with the process and less traumatised.

# Conclusion

We are entering a new paradigm in holistic birthing, and it involves emotionally intelligent delivery. It takes us out of the Western birthing model, which has seen giving birth as a mechanical process, and into an understanding that babies are emotional beings with sensory feelings.

Up until now, many of our Western medical interventions have ignored the emotions – not only in their role of creating disease but also in their role of healing it. In the last few decades, we have started to become more emotionally intelligent and this is beginning to slowly filter through to our medical processes. Progress has been slow so far, and barbaric and traumatic practices are still commonplace in the birthing room, because of our lack of awareness of their impact. These effects can impact children and still be problematic in adulthood. Since our birth is our first experience of the world, a traumatic birth can shape the belief systems and the wiring of the brain to perceive a world filled with danger, rather than a world of love. We continue to operate from these filters until they are transformed.

A host of new techniques has emerged over the past few decades that increase our emotional intelligence. One of these is Emotional Freedom Techniques (EFT), a tool that can be self-applied. It can help you release the energetic charge around a traumatic event. EFT can be used to clear the trauma from the past, so you can experience more peace in the present.

From EFT, a further tool emerged, known as Matrix Reimprinting. We explored how this tool not only takes the charge out of the emotional trauma, but enables us to rewrite it. It helps us change the pictures that we tune into subconsciously around a traumatic event, which is the single most effective way to transform our life experience in the present.

In this book we have also introduced another tool, Matrix Birth Reimprinting. I created this tool when I came to understand that the biggest filter we have on our reality is often our first experience of life. If we can recognise the impact of birth trauma on our life experience, clear the energetic charge that the trauma created, and then rewrite our birth stories, the way we show up in the world can transform dramatically.

As you begin this work, you can have profound understanding and learning of where your beliefs were originally created, but there is often more to be done around your later life experiences. You may have had a belief set up at birth that ricocheted through the rest of your life, creating a pattern with a whole host of accompanying traumatic challenges. But getting to the root of what you learnt about the world from conception, pregnancy, and childbirth, and rewriting this story, is an essential part of your healing process.

Whether there was a severe trauma or a series of lesser impacting ones, the tools that we shared in this book will enable you to rewrite your birth story. You may need a practitioner or someone versed in these tools to help you do so, but if you apply what you learnt and make a commitment to rewriting your birth, your whole reality is likely to transform. I look forward to hearing your stories of transformation as you *Heal Your Birth* and *Heal Your Life*.

# Advice from Your Younger Self

I asked some friends and colleagues what inspirational advice, from hindsight, they would give to their younger self, or ECHO, during pregnancy and birth, and here is what they shared.

> *The one thing I wish I had known before becoming a parent: that self-care and attending to my needs have to come first without guilt or shame. Being a 'mummy martyr' is a recipe for exhaustion and ill health. And if the 'mother ship' goes down, she takes everyone in the family with her. Asking for help is not a sign of failure!!* **Andie**

> *Enjoy that time, it's precious. Create magical moments during the pregnancy to look back on and it will be a wonderful memory. Be confident and trust your gut feelings.* **Rob Moon, father of three wonderful girls**

> *Trust more, be open, listen to your inner self and seek inner connection, have better self-care, don't listen to everyone who wants to share advice, slow down and enjoy the moments... even the tired ones.* **Paula Rosario**

> *I actually did tell my pregnant self that I was a different person and that I was capable of giving birth naturally. And I did.* **Rebecca Thompson**

*Follow your own parenting instincts and don't follow bad advice from health-care professionals and family members who do not have the same values as you. Get to know like-minded people. This makes ALL the difference. Really take the time to connect with the baby during pregnancy and don't be so stressed.*
**Tansy Rock**

*Take time to enjoy your children.* **Tony Stewart**

*The birth strengthens your relationship with your wife. Trust your own judgement and be yourself.* **Steve**

*It is all perfect: your biggest teacher has arrived – now be present to what is!* **John Sleeman**

*Just have confidence and be happy and keep on pedalling.*
**Nadine Atkinson**

*RELAX, give yourself more time at the labour stage and trust your body more than the midwives.* **Cara Wilde**

*Go with the flow because your body knows what to do…and breathe. Believe in yourself.* **Janet Stephan**

*Awareness of your feelings is key! You are the perfect match for both of you. Your children will be your greatest teachers!* **Sue Frend**

*It's going to hurt physically. It's going to hurt mentally. Even though it hurts, you're a physically and mentally strong enough person anyway.* **Sharon Branagh**

*Hold them and love them more. Stuff everything else!*
**Lesley Foley**

*The biggest piece of advice is to be good to yourself through the whole process and trust in your body.* **Mango Tango**

*Read books on babies and what they want, learn about conscious parenting, interact and make the baby feel more welcome than you are already doing; choose an alternative birth that will be welcoming and kind to the baby; surround yourself with many women friends who can help you with giving birth and teach you about babies and being a MUM.* **Darshana Ji**

*Release fears – fear leads to physical pain – lots of books support this idea. Enjoy your growing baby and your magical body that supports a human being coming into being.*
**Alina Frank**

*The biggest message from your younger self is to listen to yourself first.* **Natalia Iwanyckyj**

*Sleep, rest, and enjoy the joys as they balance the woes and if you consider that you stuffed up, know that you are doing your best at all times with the resources that you have at the time and that Sharon and her team are at hand to allow you to do it all over again in the matrix.* **Helen Gurnhill**

*Remember, it's never too late to have the birth of your dreams.*
**Sharon King**

# References

1   Chait, Jennifer, 'Newborn eye medication drops', *Pregnancy & Baby* April 13, 2009, www.pregnancyandbaby.com/baby/articles/932745/newborn-eye-medication-drops
    Dekker, Rebecca, PhD, RN, APRN, 'Erythromycin Eye Ointment Always Necessary for Newborns?', *Evidence Based Birth*, Nov 11, 2012, www.evidencebasedbirth.com/is-erythromycin-eye-ointment-always-necessary-for-newborns/

2   Oxford University, 'Babies feel pain "like adults"', www.ox.ac.uk/news/2015-04-21-babies-feel-pain-adults

3   Emerson, William R, PhD, 'The Vulnerable Prenate' – also published in the *Pre- and Perinatal Psychology Journal*, 10(3), Spring 1996, p.2 http://www.healyourearlyimprints.com/pdf/96_5%20Vuln%20Prenate_final.pdf

4   Emoto, Masaru, MD, www.masaru-emoto.net

5   Walsh, Becky, *You Do Know: Learning to Act on Intuition Instantly*, Hay House, London UK 2013, p.3

6   Chamberlain, David, from *The Mind of Your Newborn Baby* by David Chamberlain, published by North Atlantic Books, USA, copyright © 1998 by David Chamberlain. Reprinted by permission of publisher, pp.146-7

7   New Kids-Center, 'Pressure Points to Induce Labor', http://www.newkidscenter.com/Pressure-Points-to-Induce-Labor.html

8   Staroversky, Ivan, 'Three Minds: Consciousness, Subconscious, and Unconscious', May 2013, www.staroversky.com/blog/three-minds-conscious-subcosncious-unconscious

9   Flook, Richard, *Why Am I Sick? How to Find out What's Really Wrong Using*

*Advanced Clearing Energetics,* Hay House, London UK, 2013, p.55

10  Lipton, Bruce, 'Are You Programmed at Birth?', www.healyourlife.com/are-you-programmed-at-birth

11  Dawson, Karl, and Marillat, Kate, *Transform Your Beliefs, Transform Your Life, EFT Tapping using Matrix Reimprinting*, Hay House, London, UK, 2014, pp.18-19

12  Lake, Ricki and Epstein, Abby, *The Business of Being Born* DVD, www.thebusinessofbeingborn.com

13  Dekker, Rebecca, 'The Evidence For Doulas', Evidence Based Birth, March 2013, www.evidencebasedbirth.com/the-evidence-for-doulas/

14  Davis, Elizabeth, and Pascali-Bonaro, Debra, *Orgasmic Birth: Your Guide to a Safe, Satisfying and Pleasurable Birth Experience,* Rodale Inc, USA, 2010, p.9

15  Crews, Claudine, CPM, LM, 'Clamping of the Umbilical Cord – Immediate or Delayed – Is this really an issue?', www.midwiferyservices.org/umbilical_cord_clamping.htm

16  National Vital Statistics System, 'Birth Data', www.cdc.gov/nchs/births.htm

17  National Institutes of Health & Texas Higher Education Coordinating Board, 'Fetal Lungs Protein Release Triggers Labor to Begin' Jan 03, 2008, www.drmomma.org/2008/01/fetal-lungs-protein-release-triggers.html

18  Wikipedia, 'Spatial visualization ability,' www.en.wikipedia.org/wiki/Spatial_visualization_ability

19  Chilton Pearce, Joseph, 'The Awakening of Intelligence', from the video series *Reaching Beyond – Magical Child*, 1994, pp. 9-10, www.ttfuture.org

20  Today Parents, 'Fetuses can learn nursery rhymes from mom's voice, study finds', July 23, 2014, www.today.com/parents/fetuses-can-learn-nursery-rhymes-moms-voice-study-finds-1D79962083

21  Austin, Diana, '*Neighbours* theme learned in the womb', The *Independent*, Jan 1994, www.independent.co.uk/news/uk/neighbours-theme-learned-in-the-womb-1407223.html

22  Bumiller, Elisabeth, 'Was a Tyrant Prefigured by Baby Saddam?' *The New York Times,* May 2004, www.nytimes.com/2004/05/15/books/was-a-tyrant-prefigured-by-baby-saddam.html

23  Bumiller, Elisabeth, 'Was a Tyrant Prefigured by Baby Saddam?' *The New York Times,* May 2004, www.nytimes.com/2004/05/15/books/was-a-tyrant-prefigured-by-baby-saddam.html

24    Sonne, John, 'On Tyrants as Abortion Survivors', *Journal of Prenatal & Perinatal Psychology & Health* 19. 2 (Winter 2004): 149-167, p.7

25    Sonne, John, 'On Tyrants as Abortion Survivors', *Journal of Prenatal & Perinatal Psychology & Health* 19. 2 (Winter 2004): 149-167, p.2

26    Sonne, John, 'On Tyrants as Abortion Survivors', *Journal of Prenatal & Perinatal Psychology & Health* 19. 2 (Winter 2004): 149-167, p.3

27    *Touch The Future* newsletter, 'How Culture Shapes the Developing Brain and the Future of Humanity,' Spring 2002, p.2

28    Mendizza, Michael, 'Sensory Deprivation and the Developing Brain', p.4, www.ttfuture.org

29    Chilton Pearce, Joseph, 'The Awakening of Intelligence', from the video series *Reaching Beyond – Magical Child*, 1994, www.ttfuture.org

30    Prescott, James, PhD, and Mendizza, Michael, 'The Origins of Love and Violence', Sensory Development and the Developing Brain, Research and Prevention DVD, www.ttfuture.org

31    Prescott, James, PhD, and Mendizza, Michael, 'The Origins of Love and Violence', Sensory Development and the Developing Brain, Research and Prevention DVD, www.ttfuture.org

32    'Rock A Bye Baby', *A Time Life* Documentary (1970) www.violence.de/tv/rockabye.html

33    RMTi 'The Importance of Integrating Primal Reflexes', www.rhythmicmovement.com/en/primitive-reflexes/the-importance-of-integrating-primitive-reflexes

34    Institute of HeartMath, 'Science of The Heart: Exploring the Role of the Heart in Human Performance' http://www.heartmath.org/research/science-of-the-heart/head-heart-interactions.html pp2

35    Institute of HeartMath, 'Science of The Heart: Exploring the Role of the Heart in Human Performance' http://www.heartmath.org/research/science-of-the-heart/head-heart-interactions.html pp1

36    McCraty, Rollin PhD, Atkinson, Mike, and Bradley, Raymond Trevor, Institute of HeartMath, 'Electrophysiological Evidence of Intuition: Part 1 The Surprising Role of the Heart', pp 1 http://www.heartmath.org/research/research-publications/electrophysiological-evidence-of-intuition-part-1-the-surprising-role-of-the-heart.html

37    McCraty, Rollin PhD, Atkinson, Mike, and Bradley, Raymond Trevor, Institute of HeartMath, 'Electrophysiological Evidence of Intuition: Part 2 A System-Wide Process?' pp 1 http://www.heartmath.org/research/research-publications/electro-physiological-evidence-of-intuition-part-2-a-system-wide-process.html

38    Chilton Pearce, Joseph, 'Pregnancy, Birth & Bonding', from the video series *Reaching Beyond – Magical Child*, 1984, p.2, www.ttfuture.org

39    Chilton Pearce, Joseph, 'Pregnancy, Birth & Bonding', from the video series *Reaching Beyond – Magical Child*, 1984, p.3, www.ttfuture.org

40    Chilton Pearce, Joseph, 'The Conflict of Interest Between Biological and Cultural Imperatives', APPPAH Conference, October 03, 2003 p.8, www.ttfuture.org

41    Chilton Pearce, Joseph, 'The Conflict of Interest Between Biological and Cultural Imperatives' APPPAH Conference October 03, 2003 p.7, www.ttfuture.org

42    Chilton Pearce, Joseph, 'The Conflict of Interest Between Biological and Cultural Imperatives' APPPAH Conference October 03, 2003, p.9, www.ttfuture.org

43    HeartMath Institute, 'Science of the Heart: Exploring the Role of the Heart in Human Performance', pp 1 http://www.heartmath.org/research/science-of-the-heart/head-heart-interactions.html

44    Richardson, Holly, 'Kangaroo Care: Why Does It Work?', *Midwifery Today* Issue 44, Winter 1997, www.midwiferytoday.com/articles/kangaroocare.asp

45    Mail Foreign Service, 'Miracle mum brings premature baby son back to life with two hours of loving cuddles after doctors pronounce him dead', *Mail Online*, Aug 27, 2010, www.dailymail.co.uk/health/article-1306283/Miracle-premature-baby-declared-dead-doctors-revived-mothers-touch.html

46    McAteer, Ollie, 'Mother's heart starts beating again after baby boy brings her back to life', *Metro* News, Thursday 28 May 2015, www.metro.co.uk/2015/05/28/mothers-heart-starts-beating-again-after-baby-boy-brings-her-back-to-life-5218405/

47    Institute of HeartMath 'The Quick Coherence Technique for Adults', http://www.heartmath.org/free-services/tools-for-well-being/quick-coherence-adult.html

48    Institute of HeartMath 'The Science Behind the emWave® and Inner Balance™ Technologies', http://www.heartmath.com/science-behind-emwave/

49    Institute of HeartMath, 'Pets: Making a Connection That's Healthy for Humans', Nov 11 pp 2 http://www.heartmath.org/free-services/articles-of-the-heart/pets-making-a-connection.html

50    Hamilton, David R, PhD, *Why Kindness is Good for You*, Hay House, London, UK, 2010, pp.61-62

51    NICB, 'The Role of Prostaglandins in Labor and Delivery', 1995 Dec;22(4):973-84, www.ncbi.nlm.nih.gov/pubmed/8665768

52    Davis, Elizabeth, and Pascali-Bonaro, Debra, *Orgasmic Birth: Your Guide to a Safe, Satisfying and Pleasurable Birth Experience*, Rodale Inc, USA, 2010, pp.8-9

53    Klaus, Marshall H, MD, Kennell, John H, MD, and Klaus, Phyllis H, CSW, M.F.C.C. *Bonding: Building The Foundations of Secure Attachment and Independence*, Perseus Books, USA, 1995, p.55

54    Mizuno, K et al, 'Mother-infant skin-to-skin contact after delivery results in early recognition of own mother's milk odor', Acta Paediatr 2004; 93: 1640-5, www.ncbi.nlm.nih.gov/pubmed/15841774

55    Canadian Children's Rights Council, 'Circumcision of Males/Females', www.canadiancrc.com/Circumcision_Genital_Mutilation_Male-Female_Children.aspx

56    Goldman, Ronald, PhD, 'Circumcision Permanently Alters the Brain', Circumcision Resource Center, www.circumcision.org/brain.htm

57    Goldman, Ronald, PhD, 'Circumcision Permanently Alters the Brain', Circumcision Resource Center, www.circumcision.org/brain.htm

58    Goldman, Ronald, PhD, Circumcision Resource Center Boston Opening Statement Jan 28, 2014, www.beschneidungsforum.de/index.-php?page=Attachment&attachmentID=948&h=0130ede9dadf078e1bb45312dc6f070307de57ce

59    Goldman, Ronald, PhD, *Circumcision: The Hidden Trauma: How an American Cultural Practice Affects Infants and Ultimately Us All*, Vanguard Publications Boston, USA, 1997, p.120

60    Goldman Ronald, PhD, 'Circumcision is a trauma', Parliamentary Assembly of the Council of Europe (PACE) hearing on January 28, 2014, www.youtube.com/watch?v=Ec92eRrnWdY

61    Goldman, Ronald, PhD, Circumcision Resource Center Boston Opening Statement Jan 28, 2014, www.beschneidungsforum.de/index. page=Attach

mentpage=Attachment&attachmentID=948&h=0130ede9dadf078e1bb
45312dc6f070307de57ce

62    hbciba's Channel, www.youtube.com/watch?v=F7DgceWbsSY&feature
      =youtu.be

63    Thirteenth European Symposium on Clinical Pharmacological Evaluation
      in Drug Control, Drugs in Pregnancy and Delivery, Schlangenbad, ICP/DSE
      105m01, December, 1984, www.aims.org.uk/effectDrugsOnBabies.htm

64    Lawrence Beech, Beverley, 'Does medication administered to a woman
      in labour affect the unborn child?', Second International Conference
      of Midwives in Budapest, Hungary, Oct 27, 2004, www.aims.org.uk/
      effectDrugsOnBabies.htm

65    Yerby M, (1996), 'Managing pain in labour – Part 3: pharmacological methods
      of pain relief', *Modern Midwife*, May, pp.22-25

66    Rajan L (1994), 'The impact of obstetric procedures and analgesia/anaesthesia
      during labour and delivery on breastfeeding', *Midwifery*, Vol 10, No 2, pp.87-100

67    Weiner PC, Hogg MIJ and Rosen M (1977), 'Effects of naloxone on pethidine-
      induced neonatal depression, Part II Intramuscular naloxone', *British Medical
      Journal*, www.ncbi.nlm.nih.gov/pmc/articles/PMC1631362/pp.228-231

68    Dr Righard & Midwife Alade published in *The Lancet*, 1990 Volume 336:1105-
      07 by Lennart Righard, MD & Margaret Alade, RN, BSC, MS

69    Emerson, William R, PhD, 'Birth Trauma: The Psychological Effects of
      Obstetrical Interventions', *Journal of Prenatal & Perinatal Psychology & Health*
      13. 1 (Fall 1998): 11-44, p.6

70    Fernance, Robyn, *Being Born*, Inner Connections, Australia, 2006, p.69

71    Vinscon DC, Thomas R, Kiser T, 'Association between epidural analgesia
      during labor and fever', 1993 jun;36(6):617-22, www.ncbi.nlm.nih.gov/
      pubmed/8505604

72    Buckley, Sarah, 'Epidurals: real risks for and mother and baby', *Birth International*,
      Nov 1998, www.birthinternational.com/articles/birth/15-epidurals-real-risks-
      for-mother-and-baby

73    Fernance, Robyn, *Being Born*, Inner Connections, Australia, 2006, p.69

74    Emerson, William R, PhD, 'Birth Trauma: The Psychological Effects of
      Obstetrical Interventions', *Journal of Prenatal & Perinatal Psychology & Health*
      13. 1 (Fall 1998): 11-44, p.8

75    Lawrence Beech, Beverley, 'Does medication administered to a woman in labour affect the unborn child?', Second International Conference of Midwives in Budapest, Hungary, Oct 27, 2004, www.aims.org.uk/effectDrugsOnBabies.htm

76    Kagan, Annie, *The Afterlife of Billy Fingers: How my Bad-boy Brother Proved to Me There's Life After Death*, Hampton Roads Publishing Company Inc, Charlottesville, USA, 2013, p.48

77    Emerson, William R, PhD, 'Birth Trauma: The Psychological Effects of Obstetrical Interventions', *Journal of Prenatal & Perinatal Psychology & Health* 13. 1 (Fall 1998): 11-44, P.6

78    Emerson, William R, PhD, 'Birth Trauma: The Psychological Effects of Obstetrical Interventions', *Journal of Prenatal & Perinatal Psychology & Health* 13. 1 (Fall 1998): 11-44, p.6

79    Emerson, William R, PhD, Birth Trauma: The Psychological Effects of Obstetrical Interventions, *Journal of Prenatal & Perinatal Psychology & Health* 13. 1 (Fall 1998): 11-44, p.6

80    Fernance, Robyn, *Being Born*, Inner Connection, Australia, 2006, p.107

81    Fernance, Robyn, *Being Born*, Inner Connection, Australia, 2006, p.34

82    Emerson, William R, PhD, Birth Trauma: The Psychological Effects of Obstetrical Interventions, *Journal of Prenatal & Perinatal Psychology & Health* 13. 1 (Fall 1998): 11-44, p.14

83    Emerson, William R, PhD, Birth Trauma: The Psychological Effects of Obstetrical Interventions, *Journal of Prenatal & Perinatal Psychology & Health* 13. 1 (Fall 1998): 11-44, p.14

84    Emerson, William R, PhD, Birth Trauma: The Psychological Effects of Obstetrical Interventions, *Journal of Prenatal & Perinatal Psychology & Health* 13. 1 (Fall 1998): 11-44, p.12

85    Emerson, William R, PhD, Birth Trauma: The Psychological Effects of Obstetrical Interventions, *Journal of Prenatal & Perinatal Psychology & Health* 13. 1 (Fall 1998): 11-44, p.12

86    Fernance, Robyn, *Being Born*, Inner Connection, Australia, 2006, p.92

87    Fernance, Robyn, *Being Born*, Inner Connection, Australia, 2006, p.92

88    Spencer, Kara Maia, Craniosacral Therapy in the Midwifery Model of Care, *Midwifery Today* Issue 87, Autumn 2008, www.midwiferytoday.com/articles/cranialsacral.asp

89    Grout, Pam, *E² Nine Do-it-Yourself Energy Experiments that Prove Your Thoughts Create Your Reality*, Hay House, London, UK, 2013, pp.105-108

90    Block, Lawrence, *Write For Your Life*, HarperCollins e-books, USA, 2006, pp.77-80

91    Simkin, Penny, and Klaus, Phyllis, CSW, MFT, *When Survivors Give Birth: Understanding and Healing the Effects of Early Sexual Abuse on Childbearing Women,* Classic Day Publishing, Washington, USA, March 2004, Preface, p.1

92    Vanishing Twin Syndrome, *What to Expect*, www.whattoexpect.com/pregnancy/pregnancy-health/complications/vanishing-twin-syndrome.aspx

93    Smith Squire, Alison, 'Twin saved her sister's life in the womb after mother was told losing both babies was "inevitable"', *Mail* Online Aug 15, 2011, www.dailymail.co.uk/health/article-2026031/Twin-saved-sisters-life-womb-mother-told-losing-babies-inevitable.html

94    Braden, Gregg, 'Twin Sisters Born Prematurely', Oct 5, 2010, www.youtube.com/watch?v=jVBWdC1zeFM

95    Arms, Suzanne, *Immaculate Deception II, Myth, Magic & Birth*, Celestial Arts, California, USA, 1994, p.1

96    Fernance, Robyn, *Being Born*, Inner Connection, Australia, 2006, p.76

97    Midwife Thinking, 'Nuchal Cords: the perfect scapegoat', July 2010, www.midwifethinking.com/2010/07/29/nuchal-cords/

98    Winder, Kelly, '9 surprising facts about The Cord Around A Baby's Neck', www.bellybelly.com.au/birth/surprising-facts-about-the-cord-around-a-babys-neck#.VNOZoUviMvE

99    'Nuchal Cords: the perfect scapegoat', July 2010, www.midwifethinking.com/2010/07/29/nuchal-cords/

100   Fernance, Robyn, *Being Born*, Inner Connection, Australia, 2006, p.60

101   Epilepsy Society, 'Vagus Nerve Stimulation' www.epilepsysociety.org.uk/vagus-nerve-stimulation#.VGTKYUviMvE

102   Houser, Patrick M, 'The Science of Father Love', 2009, www.fatherstobe.org

# Picture Credits

Part and Chapter title pages alerrandre www.fiverr.com

Page 45 Robert L. Lopez KISIO Design http://kisiodesign.wix.com/kisio-design

Page 48 Sayu Gonzalez www.fiverr.com/sayugnz

Page 99 Photo courtesy of the Institute of HeartMath – https://www.heartmath.org/

Page 106 Photo courtesy of the Institute of HeartMath – https://www.heartmath.org/

Page 109 Photo courtesy of the Institute of HeartMath – https://www.heartmath.org/

Page 259 by Louise Jolley Photography

# Bibliography

Arms, Suzanne, *Immaculate Deception II, Myth, Magic & Birth*, Celestial Arts, California, USA, 1994

Axness, Marcy, *Parenting for Peace: Raising The Next Generation of Peacemakers*, First Sentient Publications, Colorado, USA, 2012

Block, Lawrence, *Write For Your Life*, HarperCollins e-books, USA, 2006

Chamberlain, David, *Babies Remember Birth: And Other Extraordinary Scientific Discoveries About the Mind and Personality of Your Newborn*, St Martins, USA, 1988

Chamberlain, David, *The Mind of Your Newborn Baby*, North Atlantic Books, California, USA, 1998

Chamberlain, David, *Windows to the Womb: Revealing the Conscious Baby from Conception to Birth*, North Atlantic Books, California, USA, 2013

Chamberlain, David, *Womb Wisdom: Awakening the Creative and Forgotten Powers of the Feminine*, Destiny Books, Vermont, USA, 2011

Childre, Doc, and Martin, Howard, *The Heartmath Solution*, HarperCollins Publishers, New York, USA, 1999

Chilton Pearce, Joseph, *Magical Child*, Bantam Books/E P Dutton, New York, USA 1977

Chilton Pearce, Joseph, *The Biology of Transcendence: A Blueprint of the Human Spirit*, Park Street Press, Vermont, USA, 2002

Chilton Pearce, Joseph, *The Crack in The Cosmic Egg: New Constructs of Mind and Reality*, Park Street Press, Vermont, USA 2002

Davis, Elizabeth, and Pascali-Bonaro, Debra, *Orgasmic Birth Your Guide to a Safe, Satisfying and Pleasurable Birth Experience*, Rodale Inc, USA, 2010

Dawson, Karl and Allenby, Sasha, *Matrix Reprinting Using EFT: Rewrite Your Past, Transform Your Future*, Hay House, London, UK, 2010

Dawson, Karl, and Marillat, Kate, *Transform Your Beliefs, Transform Your Life, EFT Tapping using Matrix Reimprinting*, Hay House, London, UK, 2014

Dick-Read, Grantly, *Childbirth Without Fear*, Pinter & Martin Ltd, London, UK, 2013

Fernance, Robin, *Being Born*, Inner Connection, Blackalls Park, Australia, 2006

Flook, Richard, *Why Am I Sick: How to Find Out What's Really Wrong Using Advanced Clearing Energetics*, Hay House, London, UK, 2013

Gaskin, Ina May, *Ina May's Guide to Childbirth*, Vermillion, USA, 2008

Gaskin, Ina May, *Spiritual Midwifery*, Book Publishing Company, Canada, 1975

Gerhardt, Sue, *Why Love Matters: How Affection Shapes a Baby's Brain*, Routledge, East Sussex, UK, 2004

Goldman, Ronald, PhD, *Circumcision The Hidden Trauma: How an American Cultural Practice Affects Infants and Ultimately Us All*, Vanguard Publications, Boston, USA, 1997

Grout, Pam, *E² Nine Do-it-Yourself Energy Experiments that Prove Your Thoughts Create Your Reality* Hay House, London, UK, 2013

Hamilton, David R, PhD, *Why Kindness is Good for You*, Hay House, London, UK, 2010

Holden, Robert PhD, *Loveability: Knowing How to Love and Be Loved*, Hay House, London, UK, 2013

Houser, Patrick, *Fathers-To-Be Handbook: A Road Map for the Transition to Fatherhood*, Creative Life Systems, USA, 2009

Kagan, Annie, *The Afterlife of Billy Fingers: How my Bad-boy Brother Proved to Me There's Life After Death*, Hampton Roads Publishing Company Inc, Charlottesville, USA, 2013

Klaus, Marshall H, MD, Kennell, John H, MD, and Klaus, Phyllis H, CSW, MFCC *Bonding: Building The Foundations of Secure Attachment and Independence*, Perseus Books, USA, 1995

Lipton, Bruce H, *The Biology of Belief: Unleashing the Power of Consciousness, Matter and Miracles*, Cygnus Books, Santa Rosa, USA, 2005

Mate, Gabor, MD, *In the Realm of Hungry Ghosts: Close Encounters with Addiction*, Random House, Canada, 2013

Moberg, Kerstin Uvnas, *The Oxytocin Factor: Tapping the Hormone of Calm, Love and Healing*, Da Capo Press, USA, 2003

Murphy Paul, Annie, *Origins: How the Nine Months Before Birth Shape the Rest of Our Lives*, Hay House, London UK, 2010

Newbigging, Sandy C, *Mind Calm: The Modern-Day Meditation Technique that Gives You 'Peace With Mind'*, Hay House, London, UK, 2014

Ortner, Nick, *The Tapping Solution: A Revolutionary System for Stress-Free Living*, Hay House, London UK, 2013

Scaer, Robert, *The Body Bears The Burden: Trauma, Dissociation and Disease*, The Haworth Medical Press, USA, 2007

Shanley, Laura Kaplan, *Unassisted Child Birth*, Praeger, California USA 2012

Simkin, Penny, and Klaus, Phyllis, CSW, MFT, *When Survivors Give Birth: Understanding and Healing the Effects of Early Sexual Abuse on Childbearing Women*, Classic Day Publishing, Washington, USA, March 2004

Thompson, Rebecca, *Consciously Parenting: What it Really Takes to Raise Emotionally Healthy Families*, The Consciously Parenting Project, USA, 2012

Thorpe, Sam, *Meta Messages from your Body: Discover the Cause of Disease and Why Your Body Doesn't Make Mistakes*, Meaningful Goals Ltd, UK

Verny, Thomas, MD, and Dr Kelly, John, *The Secret Life of the Unborn Child: A remarkable and controversial look at life before birth*, Time Warner Books, London, UK, 1981

# Resources

**Matrix Reimprinting and EFT Resources**
Matrix Reimprinting, www.matrixreimprinting.com
Matrix Birth Reimprinting, www.magicalnewbeginnings.com
The Association for Meridian & Energy Therapies (The AMT),
www.theamt.com
Association for the Advancement of Meridian Energy Techniques (AAMET),
www.aamet.org
Gary Craig, www.emofree.com
Tapping Solution, www.thetappingsolution.com
EFT Universe, www.eftuniverse.com

**Birth-Related Websites and Organisations**
APPPAH: The Association For Prenatal and Perinatal Psychology
And Health, www.birthpsychology.com
Touch The Future, www.ttfuture.org
Consciously Parenting Project – Rebecca Thompson
www.consciouslyparenting.com
Suzanne Arms, www.birthingthefuture.org
Dr Marcy Axness, www.marcyaxness.com
Mary Jackson, Ray Castellino, BeBa clinic, www.beba.org
Dr Gabor Maté, www.drgabormate.com

**Other Resources**
Access Consciousness, www.accessconsciousness.com

Colour Mirrors, www.colourmirrors.com
HeartMath Institute, www.heartmath.com
Mind Calm Meditation, www.mindcalm.com
Rhythmic Movement Training (RMT), www.rythmicmovement.com
The Masgutova Method, www.masgutovamethod.com

## DVDs

*The Origins of Love and Violence,* Sensory Development and the Developing Brain, Research and Prevention, Prescott, James PhD, Mendizza, Michael, www.ttfuture.org

*Cut: Slicing Through the Myths of Circumcision*, Ungar-Sargon, Eliyahu, http://www.cutthefilm.com

*The Living Matrix – The New Science of Healing*, Becker, Greg and Massey, Harry, www.thelivingmatrixmovie.com

*What Babies Want* Takikawa, Debbie, www.whatbabieswant.com & www.magicalnewbeginnings.com

*Giving Birth – Unveiling Birth: The Wisdom, Science and Heart,*
Arms, Suzanne, www.birthingthefuture.org

*The Business of Being Born,* Lake, Ricki and Epstein, Abby, www.thebusiness ofbeingborn.com

*Undisturbed Birth: The Science and the Wisdom,* Buckley, Sarah J, MD, www. sarahbuckley.com

*Nature, Nurture and the Power of Love the Biology of Conscious Parenting,* Lipton, Bruce, PhD, www.brucelipton.com

*Organic Birth: The Best-Kept Secret*, Pascali-Bonaro, Debra and Liem, Kris, www.organicbirthmovie.com

*The Hope-Filled Parent: Meditations for Foster and Adoptive Parents of Children who Have Been Harmed,* Trout, Michael, Available at Amazon

*Real Birth Stories: By Parents for Parents*, www.realbirthstories.com.

*Happy Healthy Child: A Holistic Approach*, www.happyhealthychild.com

*The Time is Now: Birth and the Primal Period*, Arms, Suzanne, www. birthingthefuture.org

*Amazing Talents of the Newborn: A Guide for Healthcare Professionals and Parents*, Klaus, Marshall MD and Klaus, Phyllis MFT, LMSW, www.bondingandbirth.org

*The Healing of Birth: Invitation to Intimacy* Postle, Elmer, www.fatherstobe.org

*Dunstan Baby Language: Discover the 5 Cries Every Newborn Uses to Communicate Their Everyday Needs,* Dunstan, Priscilla, www.dunstanbaby.com

*BabyBabyOhBaby, Bonding with Your Brilliant & Beautiful Baby Through Infant Massage* and *BabyBabyOhBaby, Nurturing Your Gorgeous & Growing Baby By Breastfeeding* www.babybabyohbaby.com

# Author Biography

Sharon King is the creator of Matrix Birth Reimprinting, an evolutionary protocol that enables us to rewrite our birth experience. Many experts worldwide are unified in the understanding that how we come into the world affects our emotional and physical health on a multitude of levels. Sharon shares that, by rewriting our births with this powerful tool, we are able to impact our wellbeing in many significant ways.

Sharon has worked with thousands of people all over the world to rewrite their birth stories, often with a remarkable impact on their lives in the present. She has taught practitioners how to help others transform their experience of being in utero and birth too.

She also works with pregnant women, to help them to have an empowered, natural birth, and with parents whose children experienced a birth trauma.

To find out more about Matrix Birth Reimprinting, to book a personal session and attend online courses or workshops, visit:
www.MagicalNewBeginnings.com

# FREE: Heal Your Birth, Heal Your Life Online Membership

Join our Heal Your Birth, Heal Your Life Membership Programme so you can study the tools and strategies shared in this book. It's free!

This programme includes access to training videos included in this book. You'll be guided step by step through the tapping sessions. You will have access to guided visualisations to help you clear your birth traumas. Plus bonus interviews by Sharon King and other leading birth professionals.

Join your free exclusive membership programme at this web address:
www.MagicalNewBeginnings.com/HYBmembership

Inside your online membership you will access:
• Training videos – The tapping points and how to use EFT
• Guided visualization –How to clear your birth experience
• Bonus materials and articles mentioned in the book
• Interviews with leading birth professionals such as
  Dr Marcy Axness, Patrick Houser, Rebecca Thompson
  and many more
• Special offers and discounts for future workshops!

All content is copyrighted and is only for personal transformation.

Visit  www.MagicalNewBeginnings.com/HYBmembership and join the Healing Revolution today!

Lightning Source UK Ltd.
Milton Keynes UK
UKOW04f0620150915

258655UK00003B/56/P